CW01425531

AIR CRASH INVESTIGATIONS

GHOSTS?

The Crash of Eastern Air Lines Flight 401

2

AIR CRASH INVESTIGATIONS

Over the last decades flying has become an every day event, there is nothing special about it anymore. Safety has increased tremendously, but unfortunately accidents still happen. Every accident is a source for improvement. It is therefore essential that the precise cause or probable cause of accidents is as widely known as possible. It can not only take away fear for flying but it can also make passengers aware of unusual things during a flight and so play a role in preventing accidents.

Air Crash Investigation Reports are published by official government entities and can in principle usually be down loaded from the websites of these entities. It is however not always easy, certainly not by foreign countries, to locate the report someone is looking for. Often the reports are accompanied by numerous extensive and very technical specifications and appendices and therefore not easy readable. In this series we have streamlined the reports of a number of important accidents in aviation without compromising in any way the content of the reports in order to make the issue at stake more easily accessible for a wider public.

Pete Collins, editor.

AIR CRASH INVESTIGATIONS

GHOSTS?

The Crash of Eastern Air Lines Flight 401

Pete Collins, editor.

MABUHAY PUBLISHING

AIR CRASH INVESTIGATIONS

GHOSTS?
The Crash of Eastern Air Lines Flight 401

Accident Report NTSB/AAR-73-concerning the crash of Eastern Air Lines flight 401 on December 29, 1972, near Miami, Florida.

All Rights Reserved © 2012 by Pete Collins, editor
pete_collins@yahoo.com

No part of this book may be reproduced or transmitted in any form or by any means, graphic, electronic, or mechanical, including photocopying, recording, taping, or by any information storage retrieval system, without the permission in writing from the publisher.

A Lulu.com imprint

ISBN: 978-1-300-36328-6

Content:

8

9

SYNOPSIS

An Eastern Air Lines Lockheed L-1011 crashed at 2342 eastern standard time,. December 29, 1972, approximately 18 miles west northwest of Miami International Airport, Miami, Florida. The air- craft was destroyed. There were 163 passengers and a crew of 13 aboard the aircraft; 94 passengers and 5 crewmembers received fatal. injuries. All other occupants received injuries- which ranged in severity from minor to critical.

The flight diverted from its approach to Miami International Airport because the nose landing gear position indicating system of the aircraft did not indicate that the nose gear was locked in the down position. The aircraft climbed to 2, OCO feet mean sea level and followed a clearance to proceed west from the airport at that altitude. During this time, the crew attempted to correct the malfunction and to determine whether or not the nose landing gear was extended.

The aircraft crashed into the Everglades shortly after being cleared by Miami Approach Control for a left turn back to Miami International Airport. Surviving passengers and crewmembers stated that the flight was routine and operated normally before impact with the ground.

The National Transportation Safety Board determines that the probable cause of this accident ,was the failure of the flight crew to monitor the flight instruments during the final 4 minutes of flight, and to detect an unexpected descent soon enough to prevent impact with the ground. Preoccupation with a malfunction of the nose landing gear position indicating system distracted the crew's attention from the instruments and allowed the descent to go unnoticed.

As a result of the investigation of this accident, the Safety Board has made recommendations to the Administrator of the Federal Aviation Administration.

CHAPTER 1

INVESTIGATION

History of Flight

Eastern Air Lines, Inc., Lockheed L- 1011, N31OEA, operating as Flight 401 (EAL 401), was a scheduled passenger flight from the John F. Kennedy International Airport (JFK), Jamaica, New York, to the Miami International Airport (MIA), Miami, Florida.

On December 29, 1972, the flight departed from JFK at 2120 [1] with 143 passengers and 13 crewmembers on board and was cleared to MIA in accordance with an instrument flight rules flight plan.

The flight was uneventful until the approach to .MIA. The landing gear handle was placed in the *"down"* position during the preparation for landing, and the green light, which would have indicated to. the flightcrew that the nose landing gear was fully extended and locked, failed to illuminate. The captain recycled the landing gear, but the green light still failed to illuminate.

At-2334:05, EAL 401 called the MIA tower and stated, *"Ah, tower, this is Eastern, ah, four zero one, it looks like we're gonna have to circle, we don't have a light on our nose gear yet."*

At 2334:14, the tower advised, *"Eastern four oh one heavy, roger, pull up, climb straight ahead to two thousand, go back to approach control, one twenty eight six."*

At 2334:21, ;he flight acknowledged, *"Okay, going up to two thousand, one twenty eight six. "*

At 2335:09, EAL 401 contacted MIA approach control and reported, *"All right, ah, approach control, Eastern four zero one, we're right over the airport here and climbing to two thousand feet, in fact, we've just reached two thousand feet and we've got to get a green light on our nose gear."*

At 2335:20, approach control acknowledged the flight's transmission and instructed EAL 401 to maintain 2, 000 feet mean sea level and turn to a heading of 360' magnetic. The new heading was acknowledged by EAL 401 at 2335:28.

At 2336:04, the captain instructed the first officer, who was flying the aircraft, to engage the autopilot. The first officer acknowledged the instruction.

At 2336:27, MIA approach control requested, *"Eastern four oh one, turn left heading three zero zero."* EAL 401 acknowledged the request and complied.

The first officer successfully removed the nose gear light lens assembly, but it jammed when he attempted to replace it.

At 2337:08, the captain instructed the second officer to enter the forward electronics bay, below the flight deck, to check visually the alignment of the nose gear indices. [2]

---

[1] All times herein are eastern standard, based on the 24-hour clock.

[2] Proper nose gear extension is indicated by the physical alignment of two rods on the landing gear linkage. With the nose wheelwell light illuminated, these rods may be viewed by means of an optical sight which is located in the forward electronics bay, just forward of the nose wheelwell.

13

At 2337:24, a downward vertical acceleration transient of 0.04 g caused the aircraft to descend 100 feet; the loss in. altitude was arrested by a pitchup input.

At 2337:48, approach control requested the flight to turn left to a heading of 270° magnetic. EAL 401 acknowledged the request and turned to the new heading.

Meanwhile, the flightcrew continued their attempts to free the nose gear position light lens from its retainer, without success. At 2338:34, the captain again directed the second officer to descend into the forward electronics bay and check the alignment of the nose gear indices.

At 2338:46, EAL 401 called MIA approach control and said, *"Eastern four oh one'11 go ah out west just a little further if we can here and, ah, see if we can get this light to come on here."* MIA approach control granted the request.

From 2338:56 until 2341:05, the captain and the first officer discussed the faulty nose gear position light lens assembly and how it might have been reinserted incorrectly.

At 2340:38, a half-second C-chord, which indicated a deviation of approx. 250 feet from the selected altitude, sounded in the cockpit. No crewmember commented on the C-chord. No pitch change to correct for the loss of altitude was recorded

Shortly after 2341, the second officer raised his head into the cockpit and stated, *"I can't see it, it's pitch dark and I throw the little light, I get, ah, nothing."*

The flightcrew and an Eastern Air Lines maintenance specialist who was occupying the forward observer seat then discussed the operation of the nose wheelwell light. Afterward, the specialist went into the electronics bay to assist the second officer.

At 2341:40, MIA approach control asked, *"Eastern, ah, four oh one how are things comin' along out there? "*

This query was made a few seconds after the MIA controller noted an altitude reading of 900 feet in the EAL 401 alphanumeric data block on his radar display. The controller testified that he contacted EAL 401 because the flight was nearing the airspace boundary within his jurisdiction.' He further stated that he had no doubt at that moment about the safety of the aircraft. Momentary deviations in altitude information on the radar display, he said, are not uncommon; and more than one scan on the display would be required to verify a deviation requiring controller action.

At 2341:44, EAL.401 replied to the controller's query with, *"Okay, we'd like to turn' around and come, come back in, "* and at 2341:47, approach control granted the request with; *"Eastern four oh one turn left heading one eight zero."* EAL 401 acknowledged and started the turn.

At 2342:05, the first officer said, *"We did something to the altitude."* The captain's reply was, *"What?"*

At 2342:07, the first officer asked, *"We're still at two thousand, right?"* and the captain immediately exclaimed, *"Hey, what's happening here? "*

At 2342:10, the first of six radio altimeter warning "beep" sounds began; they ceased immediately before the sound of the initial ground impact.

At 2342:12, while the aircraft was in a left bank of 28°, it crashed into the Everglades at a point 18.7.statute miles west-northwest of MIA (latitude 25° 52' N., longitude 80° 36' W.). The aircraft was destroyed by the impact.

Local weather at the time of the accident was clear, with un-restricted visibility. The accident occurred in darkness, and there was no Moon.

Two ground witnesses had observed the aircraft shortly before impact to be at an altitude that appeared low.

Injuries to Persons

Injuries	Crew	Passengers	Other
Fatal	5	94	0
Nonfatal [3]	10*)	67	0
None	0	0	0

*) Includes two nonrevenue passengers, one occupying an observer seat in the cockpit and the other seated in the, first-class section of the cabin.

The accident survivors sustained various injuries; the most prevalent were fractures of the ribs, spine, pelvis, and lower extremities. Fourteen persons had various degrees of burns; Seventeen persons received only minor injuries and did not require hospitalization:

Post-mortem examination of the captain revealed a tumor which emanated from the right side of.-the tentorium in the cranial cavity. The tumor displaced and thinned the adjacent right occipital lobe of the brain. The lesser portion of this meningioma extended downward into the superior-portion of the right cerebellar hemisphere. The tumor measured 4.3 centimeters laterally, 5.7 centimeters vertically, and 4.0 centimeters in an anterior-posterior direction.

Damage to Aircraft

The aircraft was destroyed.

---

[3] One nonrevenue passenger and one other passenger succumbed to their injuries more than 7. days subsequent to the accident. 14 CFK 430, section 430. 2, requires that these deaths be classified herein as "nonfatal."

Other Damage

None.

Crew Information

The captain, the first officer, and the second officer were certificated to serve as crewmembers for this flight. (See Appendix B for detailed information.)

An Eastern Air Lines L-101 1 maintenance specialist, one of the two nonrevenue passengers, occupied the forward observer seat during the flight from JFK.

Aircraft Information

The Lockheed L- 1011, serial No. N310EA,: was operated. by Eastern Air Lines; Inc. The aircraft was certificated, equipped, and maintained in accordance with Federal Aviation-Administration (FAA) requirements. (See Appendix C for detailed information.)

Meteorological Information

The-official surface weather observations: MIA before .and after the time of the accident were, in part, as follows:

2253 - 2,500 feet scattered visibility 10 miles, temperature 72° F.; dew point 59° F.,' - wind.80°at 7 knots altimeter setting 30. 20 inches.

2350 - 2,500 feet scattered, visibility 10 mile's, temperature 72° F., dew point 59° F, wind 080° at 8 knots, altimeter setting 30. 19 inch;.

Aids to Navigation

The flight path of the aircraft was being monitored by MIA approach control, aided by the Automated Radar Terminal Service (ARTS-III) equipment.[4]

Communications

No difficulties with communications between the flight and the air traffic control facilities were reported.

Aerodrome and Ground Facilities

Not involved.

Flight Recorders

N31 OEA was equipped with a Lockheed Aircraft Service Co. Model. 209, expandable digital flight data recorder system (DFDR), serial No. 105. This is a new type of recorder which has the capability to record numerous performance parameters on 1/4-inch magnetic tape. Recorded data are retrieved and printed out. In this case, 62 parameters were printed out. This large number of performance parameters provided the investigators a comprehensive and detailed history of flight. In addition to the normal description of the airspeed, altitude, heading, and vertical acceleration of the aircraft, availability of additional data relating to engine thrust, control surface position, roll angle, pitch attitude, angle of attack, etc., provided the basis for a comprehensive aerodynamic evaluation

---

[4]ARTS-III is a system which automatically processes the transponder beacon return from all transponder-equipped aircraft within a specific range of the approach control radar-equipment. The computed data are selectively presented on a data block next to each aircraft's updated position on the air traffic controller's radar display. The information provided to the controller is aircraft identification, groundspeed in knots, and, when the transponder of the aircraft being tracked has a special MODE C capability; pressure-altitude in 100-foot increments.

and the basis for the analysis of the autopilot and auto throttle systems.

The aircraft was also equipped with a Fairchild Model A-100 Cockpit Voice Recorder (CVR), serial No. 3125. The CVR tape was recovered intact, and a transcription was made of the voices and sounds commending at the time of the crew's initial call to the MIA Tower. (See Appendix D for details.)

Aircraft Wreckage

The terrain in the impact area was flat marshland, covered with soft mud under 6 to 12 inches of water. The elevation at the accident site was approximately 8 feet above sea level.

The left outer wing structure impacted the ground first; the No. 1 engine,. and then the left main landing gear, followed immediately. The aircraft disintegrated, scattering wreckage over an area approximately 1,600 feet long and 300 feet-wide. No complete circumferential cross-section remained of the passenger compartment of the fuselage, which was broken into four main sections and numerous small pieces. The entire left wing and left stabilizer were demolished. No evidence of in- flight structural failure, fire, or explosion was found.

The nature of the breakup precluded determination, by physical means, of the integrity of the primary flight control system before impact. The primary flight control positions were recorded, however, by the DFDR. These data show that the control columns were in an aircraft nose-up position when the crash occurred. The DFDR record depicted the spoiler positions as retracted: the three intact spoilers on the remains of the right wing were found, by inspection, to be retracted. The wing flap lever in the cockpit was set at 18O flap extension, and the extension of the inboard jackscrew on the inboard section of the right wing flap corresponded with that setting. The leading edge slat sections on the intact portion of the right wing were found fully extended. The wing flap and leading edge slat positions agreed with the DFDR record.

The landing gear lever was in the geardown position . The right main landing gear, which remained in place, was down and locked. The left main landing gear and the nose landing gear, along with portions of their attach structure, were separated from the airplane and were extensively damaged. The nose gear down-and-locked visual indicator and the nose wheelwell service light assembly were both in place and operative. The nose gear warning light lens assembly was jammed in a position that was 90° clockwise to and protruding a quarter of an inch from its normal position. Both bulbs in the unit were burned out.

Except for the altitude portion of the first officer's Air Data Computer (ADC), both ADC's and the Pitot static instruments operated satisfactorily during functional testing. The first officer's ADC sustained impact damage, and the altitude sensing portion of the unit could not be tested. The captain's ADC altitude, true airspeed, and calibrated airspeed validity flags were monitored by the DFDR. No failures were recorded.

The captain's and first officer's altimeters both indicated approximately 75 feet below sea level. The readings on the captain's airspeed and vertical speed indicators were 198 knots and 3,010 feet per minute down. The readings on the first officer's airspeed and vertical speed indicators were 197 knots and 2,950 feet per minute down. The captain's radio altimeter was set for a decision height of 30 feet, whereas the first officer's radio altimeter was set for 51 feet. The radio altimeter aural tone, which sounds during descent at 50 feet above the selected decision height, was recorded on the CVR 2 seconds before impact.

Functional tests of the captain's and first officer's attitude director indicators revealed that both units were capable of satisfactory operation.

The two autopilot-engage switches and the two flight

director system select switches were found in the "off" position. An altitude of 2, 000 feet was found selected in the altitude select window. The heading select window showed a. 180° heading selection. The vertical speed window showed a descent of 2,500 feet per minute.

Pre-impact malfunction was not evident in the examination of the aircraft hydraulic and electrical systems. Until the aircraft crashed, the DFDR recorded proper operation by the various controls and instruments which used hydraulic and electrical power.

The No. 1 engine separated from its attach structure and came to rest near its point of initial impact. The No. 2 engine remained in place, and was relatively undama.ged. The No. 3 engine separated from its attach structure and came to rest near the remains of the right wing. All engines showed evidence of leading edge damage to the fan blades, breakage of the low-pressure (LP) fan blades, or blade bending in a direction opposite to the engine rotation. All of the LP fan discs were intact and secured; operational distress was not evident. The engine pressure ratio (EPR) values of each engine were recorded by the DFDR. The record showed that the EPR values of the Nos. 1, 2, and 3 engine were 1.083, 1.073, and 1.066, respectively, at the time of ground impact.

Fire

There was no evidence of in-flight fire or explosion. After impact, a flash fire developed from sprayed fuel. Some of the burning fuel penetrated the cabin area, causing 14 passengers to suffer various degrees of burns on exposed body surfaces.

Survival Aspects

The search for the aircraft and the initial rescue efforts were coordinated by the United States Coast Guard, which was notified of the accident by Miami tower controllers. Helicopters were airborne almost immediately from the Coast Guard station at Opa-

21

Locka, Florida. The crash site was located about 15 to 20 minutes later. Despite the total darkness and the swampy condition of the site, as well as the relative remoteness of one group of survivors from another, rescue efforts were started immediately and were completed approximately 4 hours later, Sixty-eight survivors were airlifted to local hospitals.

Most of the survivors were located in the vicinity of the cockpit area, the midcabin service area, the overwing area, and the empennage section; these sections were located at the far end of the wreckage path. In contrast, most fatalities were found in the center of the crash path. Crushing injuries to the chest were the predominant causes of death.

Tests and Research

Performance tests were conducted at Miami on January 7, 1973, using the Eastern Air Lines L-1011 simulator, and on January 9, 1973, using an L- 1011 test aircraft. Before the flight tests, the computers (except the roll computers) from the accident aircraft's Avionic Flight Control System (AFCS), and a new flight data recorder were installed in the test aircraft.

In addition to the tests in Miami, the Safety Board organized an Aircraft Performance Group at the Lockheed-California Company, Palmdale, California, to analyze the aerodynamic characteristics of the Lockheed L-1011 in relation to the flight performance characteristics of the accident aircraft. The DFDR and the CVR readouts from the Miami test aircraft were used by the group in the comparative analysis. This group also conducted a collateral study of the aircraft's autopilot and auto-throttle systems, based on normal operation, to determine if they were operational during the final moments of Flight 401. This investigation disclosed the following:

1. The accident flightpath was consistent with the established aerodynamic characteristics of the L-1011.

2. The autopilot was engaged at various times during the flight, and was in the control wheel steering (CWS) pitch mode during the last 288 seconds of the flight.

3. The auto-throttle system was not in use during the final descent.

The AFCS computers were checked for operation. The computers for pitch control and auto-throttle were found operative. Subsequent flight tests of the computers in the test aircraft simulating the flightpath of Flight 401 were satisfactory.

Autoflight engage switches, altitude select controls, and speed control system selectors in the AFCS also checked satisfactory. The autopilot pitch control servo that interfaces the autopilot with the primary flight controls likewise was bench tested with satisfactory results.

The throttle control servo in the speed control system and the and throttle clutch system were tested, no discrepancies were uncovered.

The air data computers and the associated indicators were found to function satisfactorily.

The CVR showed that the radio altimeters were operating at the time the aircraft impacted the ground.

Other Information

The Lockheed L-1011 Avionic Flight Control System is composed of four major subsystems: the autopilot flight director system, the yaw stability augmentation system, the speed control system, and the flight control electronics system.

The autopilot flight director system (APFDS), which provides autopilot and flight-director pitch and steering commands, has two roll and two pitch computers. One set is designated the "A" system and the other. the "B" system.

The ."A" system relates to autopilot on the captain's side; the "A" and to the flight director. The "B" system relates to autopilot "B" and to the flight director on the first officer's side. Each pitch and roll computer has- a dual channel with a self-monitoring capability. Both autopilots cannot be operated simultaneously, except in the autoland mode. The function and operation of the autopilot are displayed on the captain's and the first officer's panels through AFCS warning and AFCS mode annuniciators. The APFDS engage panel, the Nos. 1 and 2 VHF navigation panels, the autothrottle system panel, the heading and pitch mode panel, a navigation mode panel, and the altitude select panel are all located on the glare shield; they are the means by which the various functions of the AFCS are selected.

The basic mode of autopilot system operation is control wheel steering, In this mode of operation, the autopilot provides attitude stabilization with attitude changes effected by the application of light forces to the control wheel by the crew.

The autopilot, when engaged in a command mode of operation, will provide total control of the aircraft in accordance with selected heading,. pitch, or navigational system inputs. In this mode of operation, the autopilot signals are derived from various computers and sensors in the integrated avionics flight control system.

When operating in any mode, the selected heading or pitch command function may be disengaged by an overriding 15-pound force applied to the respective, i. e., lateral or pitch, control system through the control wheel. If the force is applied to the pitch control system, only pitch axis control will be effected, reverting to the basic attitude stabilization mode of operation. If the force is applied to the roll control system, the autopilot engage lever will revert to the CWS position.

The autopilot may be completely disengaged by moving the engage lever to "OFF" or by operating a button switch on either control wheel. An additional safety feature is incorporated into the autopilot design by limiting the control wheel induced force such that a pilot may at any time manually override autopilot signals.

The altitude hold mode of operation is unique in that, although it is a command function, it may be engaged when the autopilot is selected to provide either basic CWS or Command operation. When altitude hold is selected, the autopilot provides pitch signals to maintain the altitude existing at the time of engagement. As described, pilot-applied pitch forces on the control wheel will cause disengagement of the altitude hold function, reverting the autopilot pitch channel to attitude stabilization sensitive to control wheel inputs. The autopilot engagement lever will, however, remain in the previously selected position, i. e., either CWS or command. It is possible, therefore, to disengage altitude hold without an accompanying "CMD DISC" warning appearing on the captain or first officer annunciator panels. The normal indications of such an occurrence would be only the extinguishing of the altitude mode select light on the glare shield and the disappearance of the "ALT" annunciation on both annunciator panels.

The two pitch computers in N310EA were not matched. The pitch override force required to disengage the altitude hold function in computer "A" was 15 pounds, whereas in computer "B" it was 20 pounds. As a result of the mismatch, it would be possible, with the "A" autopilot system engaged, to disengage the "A" XFCS computer, but not the "B" AFCS computer. In this situation, the altitude mode select light would remain on, the "ALT" indication on the captain's annunciator panel would go out, and the same indication on the first officer's annunciator panel would remain on, which would give the first officer the erroneous indication that the autopilot was engaged in the altitude hold mode.

CHAPTER 2

ANALYSIS AND CONCLUSIONS

Analysis

It was concluded from the investigation and the data obtained from tests, that the aircraft power-plants, airframe, electrical and Pitot static instruments, flight controls, and hydraulic and electrical systems were not factors contributing to this accident. Investigation of the Air Traffic Control responsibilities in this accident revealed another instance where the ARTS III system conceivably could have aided the approach controller in his ability to detect an altitude deviation of a transponder-equipped aircraft, analyze the situation, and take timely action in an effort to assist the flightcrew. In this instance, the controller, after noticing on his radar that the alphanumeric block representing Flight 401 indicated an altitude of 900 feet, immediately queried the flight as to its progress. An immediate positive response from the flightcrew, and the knowledge that the ARTS III equipment, at times, indicates incorrect information for up to three scans, led the controller to believe that Flight 401 was in no immediate danger. The controller continued with his responsibilities to the five other flights within his jurisdiction.

The Board recognizes that the ARTS III system was not 'designed' to provide terrain clearance information and that the

FAA has no procedures which require the controller to provide such a service. However, it would appear that everyone in the overall aircraft control system has an inherent responsibility to alert others to apparent hazardous situations, even though it is not his primary duty to effect the corrective action.

The destruction of the fuselage, with the possible exception of the cockpit area, was to such an extent that the generally accepted factors which affect occupant survivability could not be applied. Survivability in accidents generally is determined by these factors: a relatively intact environment for the occupants, crash forces which do not exceed the limits of human tolerance, adequate occupant restraints, and sufficient escape provisions. A useful distinction may, therefore, be made between impact survival and post-crash survival. Impact survival implies that the crash forces generated by the impact were of a nature which did not exceed the limits of the occupant's structural environment nor the occupant's physiological limits. Post-crash survival is determined by the occupant's successful escape from his environment before conditions become intolerable as a result of fire, water immersion, or other post-crash conditions. This requires non-incapacitation and adequate exit provisions.

From the above, it is evident that two important factors affecting impact survival were exceeded in this accident: loss of environmental protection and loss of restraint. The injuries of most of the fatalities can be attributed directly to these factors. Therefore, despite the fact that 77 occupants survived, the Board cannot place this accident in the survivable category.

The high survival rate is difficult to explain. The location of the majority of survivors near the 'larger fuselage sections would indicate that they remained with these sections until the velocity was considerably reduced or until these sections came to a stop. Although the fuselage shell was torn away, thereby exposing the occupants to external hazards, the fuselage structure apparently did not impinge on these survivors. The Board believes, therefore, that the 76 cabin occupants survived because either their seats remained attached to large floor sections or the occupants were thrown clear of the wreckage at considerably reduced velocities.

A final survival factor which deserves attention is the design of the passenger seats in this aircraft. These seats incorporated energy absorbers in the support structure. Additionally, in contrast with the conventional floor tie-down arrangement of aircraft seats, each of the seat units in this aircraft was bolted to a platform, which in turn was fitted to tracks attached to basic aircraft structure. It was noted that many of the seat units remained attached to these platforms and that failures occurred because the basic aircraft structure was compromised, rather than the platform attachments. Although many seat leg failures also were noted, these failures occurred because forces were applied in an aft direction; the seats are stressed to withstand much lower loads in the aft direction than in a forward direction. In fact, the Federal Aviation Regulations do not have a stress requirement in the aft direction for aircraft seats. The Board is of the opinion that the design of the passenger seats in this aircraft materially contributed to the survival of many occupants.

The thrust of the investigation was focused on ascertaining the reasons for the unexpected descent. The areas considered were:

1. Subtle incapacitation of the pilot.

2. The autoflight system operation.

3. Flightcrew training.

4. Flightcrew distractions.

Subtle incapacitation had to be considered in view of the finding of a tumor in the cranial cavity of the captain. The medical examiner suggested that the space-occupying lesion could have affected the captain's vision particularly where peripheral vision was concerned. Additionally, in the public hearing held in connection with this accident, expert testimony revealed that the onset of this type of tumor is slow enough to allow an individual to adapt, by compensation, to the lack of peripheral vision so that neither he nor other close associates could be aware of any changed behavior. It was also noted that the extent of peripheral vision loss, .in this case, could not be predicated with any degree of accuracy on its size and location in the cranial cavity.

It was hypothesized that if the captain's peripheral vision was severely impaired, he might not have detected movements in the altimeter and vertical speed indicators while he watched the first officer remove and replace the nose gear light lens. However, the captain's family, close friends, and fellow pilots advised that he showed no signs of visual difficulties in the performance of his duties and in other activities requiring peripheral vision. In the absence of any indications to the contrary, the Board believes that the presence of this tumor in the captain was not a causal factor in this accident.

In considering the use of the auto-flight system, it was noted that the go-around was flown manually by the first officer until 2336:04 when the captain ordered engagement of the autopilot. The affirmative reply by the first officer implies that the autopilot was engaged at this time. Verification of such action was provided by the aircraft performance group analysis of the DFDR readout which showed pitch control surface motions indicative of autopilot control in either altitude hold or pitch CWS.[5] Which of the autopilots was

---

[5] It was concluded that the autopilot was engaged at various times throughout the flight from JFK. A complete mode assessment summary for the pertinent portions of the 27-minute period preceding impact is contained in Appendix G. In attempts to distinguish between autopilot "ON" and "OFF," considerable reliance was placed on DFDR data which showed the ratio between pilot and copilot control cable system input motion in the roll axis, since the ratio varies between manual and autopilot operation. This characteristic of the L- 1011 lateral control system, verified by ground and flight tests, was used to distinguish between autopilot "ON" and "OFF" whenever there was appreciable roll activity. , During lateral maneuvering with CWS, this ratio becomes less definitive, and, although autopilot "OX" and "OFF" status can be determined, positive identification of the selected mode becomes more difficult-

engaged, i.e., system "A" or system "B, " could not be determined. Testimony by pilots at the public hearing indicated that the first officer would have probably engaged system "B" to the command position with the altitude hold and heading select functions selected, in accordance with general practices. At the same time, the first officer probably selected 2, 000 feet into the altitude select/alert panel.

At approximately 2337, some 288 seconds prior to impact, the DFDR readout indicates a vertical acceleration transient of 0. 04 g causing a 200-f.p.m. rate of descent. For a pilot to induce such a transient, he would have to intentionally or inadvertently disengage the altitude hold function. It is conceivable that such a transient could have been produced by an inadvertent action on the part of the pilot which caused a force to be applied to the control column. Such a force would have been sufficient to disengage the altitude hold mode. It was noted that the pitch transient occurred at the same time the captain commented to the second officer to *"Get down there and see if the nose wheel's down."* If the captain had applied a force to the control wheel while turning to talk to the second officer, the altitude hold function might have been accidentally disengaged. Such an occurrence could have been evident to both the captain and first officer by the change on the annunciator panel and the extinguishing of the, altitude mode select light. If-autopilot system "A" were engaged, however, the discrepancy in the disengage force comparators, i.e., the mismatch between computers "A" and "B" would become a significant factor in this analysis. Because of this mismatch and the system design, a force eserted on the captain's control wheel in excess of 15 pounds, but less than 20 pounds, could result in disengagement of the altitude hold function without the occurrence of a corresponding indication of the first officer's annunciator panel. This would lead to a situation in which the first officer, unaware that altitude hold had been disengaged, would not be alerted to the aircraft altitude deviation. If the autopilot system "B" was engaged, as is believed to have happened, such a situation could not have occurred since a force in excess of 20 pounds would have been required to disengage the altitude hold function and both annunciator panels would have indicated correctly. Therefore, the Board concludes that the mismatched pitch computers in the auto-flight system were not a critical factor in this accident.

However, it is significant that recognition of the aforementioned 100-foot loss took 30 seconds after the 0. 04 g pitch transient occurred, and after a heading change was requested by approach control. The DFDR readout indicates a 0.9° pitchup maneuver coincident with a change of heading. It was concluded from the DFDR analysis of lateral control system motions that the heading select mode was used for the last 255 seconds of flight to control the aircraft to a heading of 270°. Since selection of the new heading would have required action by the first officer, which included attention to the autopilot control panel, it is reasonable to assume that he should have been aware of the selected heading select functions at this time. It is also reasonable to assume that the autopilot was set up to provide pitch attitude stabilization sensitive to control wheel inputs and heading select, wherein lateral guidance signals were provided to achieve and maintain the 270° heading.

In the pitch attitude stabilization mode, the aircraft will respond to intentional or unintentional movements of the control wheel. Furthermore, while the aircraft is operating in this mode, the effect of aircraft thrust changes, without compensating pitch attitude control inputs, will be directly related to changes in vertical speed.

A series of reductions in power began 1.60 seconds before impact. The power reductions and slight nose-down pitch control movements together were responsible for the unrecognized descent which followed. Extensive flight testing and simulation studies of N310EA's entire Speed Control System (SCS) (auto-throttle) were conducted to identify the reason for the series of reductions in thrust during the last few minutes of the flight. Thrust reductions generated by the N310EA autothrottle components installed in the test aircraft were dissimilar to those reductions recorded on the DFDR from the accident aircraft. In one series of flight tests, the autothrottle speed reference was set to 175 knots indicated airspeed (IAS);and a descent rate of 200 feet per minute was established. The airspeed was maintained to within approx. 3 knots of the reference speed by the SCS, until the autothrottle authority limits were reached (flight idle thrust). Such control during the flight of N301EA was not evident; a 15-knot increase in airspeed did occur, with throttle authority still available. Comparison of the autothrottle system simulation data with Flight 401's airspeed and acceleration data confirmed that the throttles would have been retarded to the flight idle position relatively quickly.

Reference to the DFDR shows that power on the No. 3 engine was increased slightly, 1 minute before reduction of power on the Nos. 2 and 3 engines (the initiation of the descent profile). This is a normal manual adjustment typically made by a pilot, and cannot be accomplished by the autothrottle system. Additionally, the speed found set on the autothrottle selector dial was 160 knots, a speed well below that attained or maintained during the last 4 minutes of flight.

An indication that the throttles were not retarded by a properly operating autothrottle system is the sequence in which the power was reduced. The first power reduction occurred on the Nos. 2 and 3 engines 160 seconds before impact. In the second reduction, the power on the No. 1 engine was matched with the power on the Nos. 2 and 3 engines. Finally, the power on the No. 1 engine was retarded for more than 10 seconds before reduction of power in the two other engines. The throttles were clutched together and driven simultaneously by one servo. If the autothrottle system was "on, " only intermittent and random failures in the clutch system would have produced asymmetrical reduction of power similar to that typical of manual throttle movement. Since the autothrottle system of N310E-4 was found to have been functional, the Board does not believe that this system was involved in the reduction of thrust.

Another explanation of the thrust reductions would seem to

be one of two alternatives -- either an inadvertent or an intentional action by one or both of the pilots. The captain might have inadvertently bumped the throttles with his right arm when he leaned over the control pedestal to assist the first officer. Similarly, the first officer's left arm might have accidentally bumped the throttles while he was occupied with the nose gear indicating system. Because the EPR reductions reflected by the DFDR do even out, at times, one of the pilots might have noted an uneven EPR display (which usually accompanies movement of a throttle), and his reaction might have been to reposition the throttle without reference to the flight instruments.

The other alternative is that one of the pilots intentionally reduced thrust power when he noted that the speed of the aircraft was exceeding the desired speed (160- 170 knots) for the flight regime involved . The intentional adjustment, similarly, most probably was made with reference to the airspeed indicators only. The crew relied on the autoflight system to maintain the aircraft's altitude, it is conceivable that a correction in airspeed might have been made without reference to other instruments. Of the two possibilities , the Board believes that the throttles were intentionally retarded by one or both of the pilots.

Regardless of the way in which the status of the autoflight system was indicated to the flightcrew, or the manner in which the thrust reduction occurred, the flight instruments (altimeters, vertical speed indicators, airspeed indicators, pitch attitude indicators, and the autopilot vertical speed selector) would have indicated abnormally for a level-flight condition. Together with the altitude-alerting, 1/2-second, C-chord signal, the flight instrument indications should have alerted the crew to the undesired descent.

The throttle reductions and control column force inputs which were made by the crew, and which caused the aircraft to descend, suggest that crewmembers were not aware of the low force gradient input required to effect a change in aircraft attitude while in CWS. The Board learned that this lack of knowledge about the capabilities of the new autopilot was not limited to the flightcrew of Flight 401. Pilot training and autopilot operational policies were studied extensively during the field phase of the investigation, and were discussed, at great length, in the public hearing connected with this accident. Although formal training provided adequate opportunity to become familiar with this new concept of aircraft control, operational experience with the autopilot was limited by company policy. Company operational procedures did not permit operation of the aircraft in CWS; they required all operations to be conducted in the command modes. This restriction might have compromised the ability of pilots to use and understand the unique CWS feature of the new autopilot

However, the Board believes that the present Eastern Air Lines training program is adequate but is in need of more frequent quality control progress checks of the student during the ground school phase of the training and an early operational proficiency follow-up check in the flight simulator after the pilot has flown the L-1011 in scheduled passenger service.

Another problem concerns the new automatic systems which are coming into service with newer aircraft and being added to older aircraft. Flightcrews become more reliant upon the functioning of sophisticated avionics systems, and their associated to fly the airplane. This is increasingly so as the reliability of such equipment improves. Basic control of the aircraft and supervision of the flight's progress by instrument indications diminish as other more pressing tasks in the cockpit attract attention because of the overreliance on such automatic equipment.

Pilots' testimony indicated that dependence on the reliability and capability of the autopilot is actually greater than anticipated in its early design and its certification. This is particularly true in the cruise phase of flight. However, in this phase of flight, the autopilot is not designed to remain correctly and safely operational, without performance degradation, after a significant failure occurs.

In any event, good pilot practices and company training dictate that one pilot will monitor the progress of the aircraft at all times and under all circumstances.

The Board is aware of the distractions that can interrupt the routine of flight. Such distractions usually do not affect other flight requirements because of their short duration or their routine integration into the flying task, However, the following took place in this accident:

1. The approach and landing routine was interrupted by an abnormal gear indication.

2. The aircraft was flown to a safe altitude, and the autopilot was engaged to reduce workload, hut positive delegation of aircraft control was not accomplished.

3. The nose gear position light lens assembly was removed and incorrectly reinstalled.

4. The first officer became preoccupied with his attempts to remove the jammed light assembly.

5. The captain divided his attention between attempts to help the first officer and orders to other crewmembers to try other approaches to the problem.

6. The flightcrew devoted approximately 4 minutes to the distraction, with minimal regard for other flight requirements.

It is obvious that this accident, as well as others, was not the final consequence of a single error, but was the cumulative result of several minor deviations from normal operating procedures which triggered a sequence of events with disastrous results.

Conclusions

(a) Findings

1. The crew was trained, qualified, and certificated for the operation.

2. The aircraft was certificated, equipped, and maintained in accordance with applicable regulations.

3. There was no failure or malfunction of the structure, powerplants, systems, or components of the aircraft before impact, except that both bulbs in the nose landing gear position indicating system were burned out.

4. The aircraft struck the ground in a 28° left bank with a high rate of sink.

5. There was no fire until the integrity of the left wing fuel tanks was destroyed after the impact.

6. The tumor in the cranial cavity of the captain did not contribute to the accident.

7. The autopilot was utilized in basic CWS.

8. The flightcrew was unaware of the low force gradient input required to effect a change in aircraft attitude while in CWS .

9. The company training program met the requirements of the Federal Aviation Administration.

10. The three flight crewmembers were preoccupied in an attempt to ascertain the position of the nose landing gear.

11. The second officer, followed later by the jump seat occupant, went into the forward electronics bay to check the nose gear down position indices.

12. The second officer was unable visually to determine the position of the nose gear.

13. The flightcrew did not hear the aural altitude alert which sounded as the aircraft descended through 1,750 feet m. s.l.

14. There were several manual thrust reductions during the final descent.

15. The speed control system did not affect the reduction in thrust.

16. The flightcrew did not monitor the flight instruments. during the final descent until seconds before impact.

17. The captain failed to assure that a pilot was monitoring the progress of the aircraft at all times.

(b) Probable Cause

The National Transportation Safety Board determines that the probable cause of this accident was the failure of the flightcrew to monitor the flight instruments during the final 4 minutes of flight, and to detect an unexpected descent soon enough to prevent impact with the ground. Preoccupation with a malfunction of, the nose landing gear position indicating system distracted the crew's attention from the instruments and allowed the descent to go unnoticed.

Recommendations

As a result of the investigation of this accident, the Safety Board on April 23, 1973, submitted three recommendations (A-73-1 1 through 13) to the Administrator of the Federal Aviation Administration: .Copies of the recommendation letter and the Administrator's response thereto are included in Appendix H.

Recommendations concerning the crash survival aspects of this accident have been combined with those of two other recent accidents and were submitted to the FAA on June 15, 1973. (See Appendix I)

The Board further recommends that the Federal Aviation Administration:

Review the ARTS III program for the possible development of procedures to aid flightcrews when marked deviations in altitude are noticed by an Air Traffic Controller. (Recommendation A-73-46.)

The Board is aware of the present rulemaking proceedings initiated by the Flight Standards Service on April 18 concerning the required installation of Ground Proximity Warning Devices. However, in view of this accident and of previous recommendations on this subject made by this Board, we urge that the Federal Aviation Administration expedite its rulemaking proceedings.

APPENDIXES

APPENDIX A: INVESTIGATION AND HEARING

Investigation

The National Transportation Safety Board received notification of the accident at 0025 eastern standard time on December 30, 1972, from the Federal Aviation Administration. An investigation team was dispatched immediately to the scene. Investigative groups were established for Operations, Air Traffic Control, Witnesses, Weather, Human Factors, Structures, Powerplants, Systems, Flight Data Recorder, and Cockpit Voice Recorder. An Aircraft Performance Group was formed at the Lockheed-California Company's flight test facility in Palmdale, California.

The Federal Aviation Administration, Eastern Air Lines, Lockheed- California Company, Rolls-Royce (1971) Limited, the Air Line Pilots Association, and the Air Line Stewards and Stewardesses Association participated and assisted the Board in this investigation.

Hearing

A public hearing was held at the Miami Springs Villas, Miami 'Springs, Florida, March 5 through March 9, 1973. Federal Aviation Administration, Eastern Air Lines, Inc., Lockheed-California Company; Air-Line Pilots Association, 'and the Aviation Consumer Action Project were parties to the hearing.

Preliminary Report

A preliminary report of the investigation was released by the Safety Board on January-11, 1973.

APPENDIX B: AIRMAN INFORMATION

Captain Robert A. Loft, aged 55, was employed by Eastern Air Lines on September 20, 1940. He received his Airline Transport Rating on July 15, 1942, and was promoted to captain on February 8, 1951. Captain Loft qualified for the DC-8 on March 13, 1969. He completed his L-1011 simulator check on April 20, 1972, and his aircraft flight check on June 7, 1972. Both checks were observed by an FAA inspector. Captain Loft's ground school instructor rated him satisfactory for the entire 8 days of his L-1011 training. Captain Loft received 2 hours and 30 minutes of flight training in the L-1011 aircraft. He completed his rating ride in 1 hour and 30 minutes. His initial line check was completed on July 1, 1972. The officer giving the flight check stated, in part, in his comments, *"Good knowledge of aircraft and procedures."* Captain Loft's last first-class medical certificate was issued on November 21, 1972, with the limitation that *"The holder shall possess correcting glasses for near vision."*

First Officer Albert J. Stockstill, aged 39, was employed by Eastern Air Lines on August 7, 1959, as a Flight Engineer. He had prior experience as an Air Force pilot. First Officer Stockstill completed his Second-in-Command training in the DC-8 on December 13, 1971. He began his L-1011 training on March 6, 1972. He completed his oral check on March 15, 1972, and his transition check on March 27, 1972; both were satisfactory. On June 1, 1972, he satisfactorily completed his First Officer qualification, which included Category III-A maneuvers. First Officer Stockstill's last first-class medical certificate was issued on April 11, 1972, with no limitations.

Second Officer Donald A. Repo, aged 51, was employed by Eastern Air Lines on September 11, 1947, as an aircraft mechanic prior to attendance at an Eastern Air Lines flight engineer school. On November 19, 1955, he qualified for his Flight Engineer Certificate, and on April 13, 1967, he qualified for his Commercial Pilot Certificate, with airplane single-engine land and instrument privileges. He began his L-1011 training on September 18, 1972. He completed his oral examination on September 29, 1972, and his simulator check on October 5, 1972. On October 3, 1972, he received a 1-1/2 hour walk around of L-1011, N31OEA. On October 7, 1972, Second Officer Repo completed his aircraft check, which included the emergency and abnormal procedures associated with the hydraulic systems and the 'landing gear. On December 19, 1972, he completed his line check. His last second-class medical certificate was issued on August 10, 1972, with the limitation that *"The holder shall possess correcting glasses for near vision. "*

The following is a listing of pertinent flightcrew information:

Item	Capt. Loft	F/O Stockstill	S/O Repo
Age	55	39	51
Date of birth	3/17/17	6 9/33	5/10/21
Time L-1011	280 hrs.	306 hrs.	53 hrs,
Total time	29, 700 hrs.	5,800 hrs.	15, 700 hrs.
Certificates	ATR	ATR & FE	FE, A&P & Commercial
Numbers	ATR-464-38	ATR-1311877 FE- 1547248	FE-1752585 Comm. -13278 A&P-291 795
Ratings	AMEL, DC-3-4, 6, 7, 8, M202, 404, L-49, L-188 L-1011 B-751/720 CW-46	AMEL, DC-3 Comm. Priv. ASEL. FE - DC-7, L-188 B-727	Comm. Priv. ASEL & Inst. F E - Recip. Turbo Prop & Turbo Jet
Hours flown 24 hrs. prior this flight	2:25	2 25	5:oo
Hours flown this flight	2:22	2 22	2:22

Item	Capt. -Loft	F/O Stockstill	S/O Repo
Duty time last 24 hrs.	9:52	9:52	9:52
Rest 24 hrs. prior to accident	14:08	14:08	14:08

All 10 flight attendants were qualified in accordance with existing regulations.

APPENDIX C: AIRCRAFT HISTORY

Aircraft N310EA, a Lockheed L-1011-385-1, serial No. N193A- 1011, was operated by Eastern Air Lines, Inc., and registered to the Manufacturers National Bank of Detroit, Michigan. It was received by Eastern Air Lines on August 18, 1972, and placed into scheduled service on August 21, 1972. At the time of the accident, it had accumulated 986 hours and 502 landings. Scheduled maintenance was accomplished by "A" (line) and "C" (major) phase checks.

The aircraft had accumulated 132 hours and 69 landings since the last "C" check and 19 hours and 10 landings since the last "A" check. The aircraft was equipped with three Rolls-Royce, RB 21 l-22C, engines. Engine serial numbers and times were as follows:

Engine Location	Date Installed	Serial Number	TSO Hours	Flight Cycles	Hours Since Installed	Cycles Since Installed
1	10-30-72	10071	807	403	407	252
2	12-14-72	10072	1144	632	130	68
3	12-S-72	10061	711	686	164	104

The weight and balance manifest for this flight indicated that the aircraft was within its weight and balance limitations both at takeoff and at the time of the accident.

There were 85, 000 pounds of fuel aboard the aircraft upon departure from New York. The planned fuel burn-off for the flight to Miami was 42, 000 pounds.

From October 17, 1972, to November 14, 1972, N310EA was used for the installation and testing of modified Fault Isolation Monitoring (FM) equipment under operating conditions. Fault Isolation Monitoring is the system used on the L-101 1 aircraft's Avionic Flight Control System to identify detected faults within the autopilot system. A complete set of modified AFCS computers was installed in the aircraft on October 29, 1972, to evaluate the revised FM circuitry. On November 14, 1972, the modified FM equipment was removed, and the original AFCS computers were reinstalled in the aircraft.

Company records indicated that N310EA had been maintained in accordance with company procedures and with FAA requirements.

Investigation revealed that N310EA was equipped with mismatched autopilot pitch computers. The "A" system pitch computer would revert from altitude hold to control wheel steering with only 15 pounds of pitch pressure on either control wheel. The "B" system, however, would not revert until it sensed 20 pounds of pressure. On July 15, 1972, Lockheed Service Bulletin No. 093-22-012 (nonmandatory-) was issued, calling for the modification of pitch computers, which changed the 20-pound release value to a 15-pound release value.

APPENDIX D: FLIGHT PROFILE

This appendix was unreadable.

APPENDIX E: WRECKAGE DISTRIBUTION CHART

This appendix was unreadable.

APPENDIX F: FLIGHTPATH SUMMARY

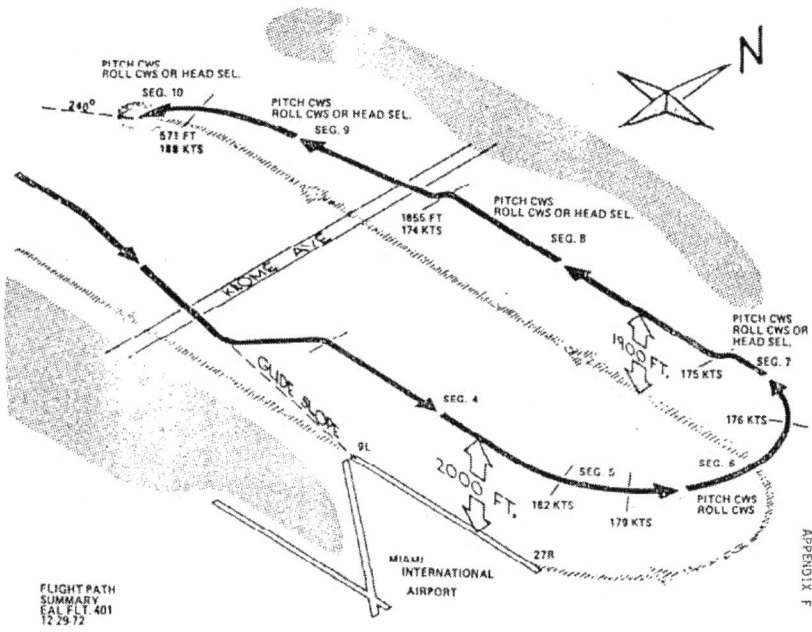

FLIGHT PATH SUMMARY
EAL FLT. 401
12 29 72

APPENDIX G: MODE ASSESMENT SUMMARY

MODE ASSESSMENT SUMMARY

SEGMENT	TIME BEFORE IMPACT	MANEUVER	OFI	PITCH CKS	ALTITUDE CAPT/HOL	VERTICAL SPEED	ROLL CWS	HEADING SELECT
1	27 min. to 20.6 min.	Descent to 9700 feet altitude		X			*	*
2	20.6 min. to 19.3 min.	Altitude Capture at 9700 feet altitude			X		*	*
3	19.3 min. to 16.3 min.	Level flight at 9700 feet altitude	X					
4	420 sec. to 373 sec.	Level out at 2000 feet altitude	#	#			#	
5	373 sec. to 355 sec.	Period before Autopilot engage order	#	#	#	#	#	
6	355 sec. to 278 sec.	Period after autopilot engage order; left turn with 12° roll angle		*pre X after 288 sec.	*pre 288 sec.		X	
7	270 sec. to 220 sec.	Acquire heading of 270°		X			X pre after 256 sec.	*after 256 sec.
8	220 sec. to 140 sec.	None - constant heading		X			*	*
9	140 sec. to 20 sec.	Pitch over and descent		X			*	*
10	20 to 0 sec.	Left turn toward 180°; Impact		X			*	*

‡‡‡ THE X DENOTES THE MODE ENGAGED AS INDICATED BY THE PERFORMANCE ANALYSIS.
THE * DENOTES EITHER OF TWO MODES INDICATED.
THE # DENOTES POSSIBLE MODES WHEN MORE THAN TWO ARE POSSIBLE.

APPENDIX H: NTSB Safety Recommendations A-73-11 thru 13

UNITED STATES OF AMERICA

NATIONAL TRANSPORTATION SAFETY BOARD
WASHINGTON, D.C.

ISSUED: May 2, 1973

Adopted by the NATIONAL TRANSPORTATION SAFETY BOARD
at its office in Washington, D. C.
on the   11th day of April 1973

FORWARDED TO:)
Honorable Alexander P. Butterfield)
Administrator   )
Federal Aviation Administration   )
Washington, D. C. 20591   )
)

SAFETY RECOMMENDATIONS A-73-11 thru 13

The National Transportation Safety Board's current investigation of
a fatal air carrier accident involving an Eastern Air Lines, Inc., L-1011,
N310EA, which crashed near Miami, Florida, on December 29, 1972, has
revealed two areas in which we believe early corrective action is needed
to prevent the recurrence of similar accidents.

The airplane involved crashed about 6 minutes after the crew had
executed a missed approach in order to check the status of the nose gear.
The green, gear-safe annunciator light had failed to illuminate when the
gear handle was placed in the gear-down position during the initial approach.

Our investigation indicates that at the time of the accident, all
three flight crewmembers were engrossed in an attempt to ascertain whether
the landing gear was safely extended, and they were not aware until just
before impact that the airplane had departed the 2,000-foot clearance altitude. The flight engineer was in the forward avionics center, located
beneath the cockpit floor and just forward of the nose wheelwell, attempting
to ascertain visually, by means of an optical sight tube, whether the gear
was locked down.

The flight engineer was not successful in his attempt to view the
rods on the nose landing gear linkage which indicate whether the gear is
locked down. If this is to be done at night, a light in the nose wheelwell
must be turned on by a switch on the captain's eyebrow panel. The person
who attempts to view the indicator rods must pull a knob located over an
optical sight in order to remove a cover on the far end of the sight. In
this case, the flight engineer twice noted that he could see nothing -- that
it was "pitch dark." We do not know whether (1) the captain ever attempted

Honorable Alexander P. Butterfield

to turn on the light (the crew seemed to think that the light should be on whenever the landing gear was extended), (2) the light was inoperative, or (3) the flight engineer properly operated the knob which removes the optical tube cover. In any event, the Safety Board believes that this unsuccessful attempt to ascertain whether the nose landing gear was locked down contributed to the distraction of the flightcrew during this flight. For this reason, the Safety Board believes that this system should be operable by one man; therefore, the switch for the wheelwell light should be located near the optical sight. Furthermore, a placard outlining the proper use of the system should be installed near the light switch and the knob for the optical sight cover.

The reason for the descent from an altitude of nearly 2,000 feet has not yet been determined. The cockpit voice recorder (CVR) indicates, however, that the altitude select, alert system sounded shortly after the initial descent. This alert system is comprised of a single C-chord and a flashing amber alert light. When the airplane departs the selected altitude by ± 250 feet, the C-chord sounds once, and the amber light flashes continuously. However, on the Eastern Air Lines configuration, this light is inhibited from operating below 2,500 feet radar altitude. Thus, on the accident airplane, the only altitude alert system warning to the crew that the airplane was descending was the single C-chord. There is no evidence on the CVR to indicate that the crew ever heard the audible warning as the airplane maintained a continuous descent into the ground.

Therefore, the Safety Board recommends that the Federal Aviation Administration:

1. Require the installation of a switch for the L-1011 nose wheelwell light near the nose gear indicator optical sight.

2. Require, near the optical sight, the installation of a placard which explains the use of the system.

3. Require that the altitude select alert light system on Eastern Air Lines-configured L-1011 airplanes be modified to provide a flashing light warning to the crew whenever an airplane departs any selected altitude by ± 250 feet, including operations below 2,500 feet radar altitude.

Members of our Bureau of Aviation Safety will be available for consultation in the above matter if desired.

Honorable Alexander P. Butterfield

These recommendations will be released to the public on the issue date shown above. No public dissemination of the contents of this document should be made prior to that date.

Reed, Chairman; McAdams, Thayer, Burgess, and Haley, Members, concurred in the above recommendations.

By: John H. Reed
Chairman

APPENDIX I: NTSB Safety Recommendations
A-73-39 thru 43

DEPARTMENT OF TRANSPORTATION
FEDERAL AVIATION ADMINISTRATION

WASHINGTON, D.C. 20590

OFFICE OF
THE ADMINISTRATOR

May 14, 1973

Honorable John H. Reed
Chairman, National Transportation Safety Board
Department of Transportation
Washington, D. C.   20591

Dear Mr. Chairman:

This replies to your Safety Recommendation A-73-11 thru 13
issued May 2, 1973, concerning modifications to preclude the
recurrence of an accident such as the Eastern Air Lines, Inc.,
L-1011, N310EA, which crashed near Miami, Florida, on
December 29, 1972.

We are studying the recommendations and will advise what actions
will be taken as soon as our evaluation is completed.

Sincerely,

Gustav E. Lundquist

Gustav E. Lundquist
Acting Administrator

UNITED STATES OF AMERICA
NATIONAL TRANSPORTATION SAFETY BOARD
WASHINGTON, D.C.

ISSUED: June 25, 1973

Adopted by the NATIONAL TRANSPORTATION SAFETY BOARD
at its office in Washington, D. C.
on the 6th   day of June 1973

FORWARDED TO:)
  Honorable Alexander P. Butterfield
  Administrator   .)
  Federal Aviation Administration)
  Washington, D. C. '20591   )
)

SAFETY RECOMMENDATIONS A-73-39 thru 43

The National Transportation Safety Board has under investigation, three accidents involving: a United Air Lines Boeing 737 at Midway Airport, Chicago, Illinois, on December 8, 1972; a North Central Airlines DC-9, at O'Hare International Airport, also at Chicago, Illinois, on December 20, 1972; and an Eastern Air Lines Lockheed L-1011 at Miami, Florida, on December 29, 1972.

The Safety Board has identified several areas in occupant survival and evacuation common to these accidents which it believes merit remedial action by the Federal Aviation Administration. These areas are delineated below:

Shoulder Harness Restraint. Testimony at the Safety Board's public hearing concerning the United B-737 accident revealed that crew takeoff and before-landing checklists did not contain the item 'Shoulder harness Fastened." The injuries sustained by the captain, as well as the conditions of the captain's and first officer's shoulder harness in the wreckage, indicated that the shoulder harness had not been used.

In the EAL accident, we noted that the shoulder harness on the aft facing cabin attendant seats had been removed. In a letter dated March 12, 1973, the Board, in commenting on your Notice of Proposed Rule Making 73-1, expressed its concern about the absence of a requirement to have shoulder harnesses installed on aft facing seats. We pointed out that in crashes or emergency landings involving multidirectional inertia forces, shoulder harnesses would provide an additional,

and possibly vital, measure of protection for occupants of aft facing
seats. The principal advantage of a shoulder harness, both in forward
and rearward facing seats, is that it helps to restrain the user in
an upright position, thereby keeping the spinal column in a more suit-
able position from the standpoint of load distribution. Additionally,
the shoulder harness prevents the upper body from flailing, a frequent
cause of serious injuries in aircraft accidents. The Board believes
that increased protection from injury of the flightcrew as well as the
cabin attendants is of vital importance, since their availability to
guide and aid passengers during evacuation may make the difference
between survival and disaster. Therefore, the Safety Board recommends
that the Federal Aviation Administration:

1. Take the necessary steps to ensure that all air carrier
   before-landing and takeoff checklists contain a "Fasten
   Shoulder Harnesses" item.

2. Amend 14 CFR 25.785(h) to require provisions for a
   shoulder harness at each cabin attendant seat, and
   amend 14 CFR 121.321 to require that shoulder harnesses
   be installed at each cabin attendant seat.

Auxiliary Portable Lighting. During the investigation and public hearing held in connection with the EAL L-1011 accident, testimony indicated
chat the absence of lighting of any kind at the crash scene seriously
hampered survivors' ability to orient themselves and prevented them
from searching for and assisting other injured survivors. Additionally
this lack of light prevented cabin attendants from taking effective
charge among the surviving passengers. In both Chicago accidents, a
similar lighting problem was encountered. Although section 121.549(b)
of the Federal Aviation Regulations requires each crewmember to have
available a flashlight, cabin attendants usually stow their personal
flashlights in their handbags, which tend to become lost in the debris
of the wreckage. This, for example, was the case in both Chicago
accidents. The Board believes that effective alternate means of lighting, which is not dependent on random stowage and location, should be
readily accessible to the flight attendants. Therefore, the Safety
Board recommends that the Federal Aviation Administration:

3. Amend 14 CFR 25.812 to require provisions for the stowage of a portable, high-intensity light at cabin attendant Stations; and amend 14 CFR 121.310 to require the
   installation of such portable, high-intensity lights at
   cabin attendant stations.

Emergency Lighting. Evidence obtained during the investigation of the North Central DC-9 accident and the United B-737 accident in Chicago, indicated that many passengers had difficulties in escaping from the wreckage. These difficulties were a result of inadequate illumination, combined with a heavy smoke condition in one of these accidents. In the United accident, survivors specifically mentioned the absence of any light in the cabin. In the North Central accident, passengers experienced great difficulty in locating the exits, reportedly because of darkness and heavy smoke in the cabin. Yet, the crew testified that the emergency lighting system was armed, and th2 inves tigation indicated that they should have been operational. However, four of the nine fatally injured passengers apparently died while they were attempting to find an exit. On2 passenger was found in the cockpit, one near the cockpit door, and two others were found near the aft end of the cabin. The five remaining fatalities apparently had not left their seats.

Numerous recommendations and proposals to improve occupant escape capabilities in survivable accidents have been made over the years by various Government and industry organizations; and, indeed, significant improvements have occurred. Unfortunately, however, experience indicates that the existing escape potential from aircraft in which postcrash fire is involved is still marginal. These accidents illustrate the vital role that adequate illumination can play in contributing to such postcrash survivability.

A review of 14 CFR 25.811 and 25.812 indicates that paragraph 811(c) requires means to assist occupants in locating exits in conditions of dense smoke. Yet, information from the Civil Aeromedical Institute in Oklahoma City indicates that the illumination levels specified in paragraph 812 are not predicated on a smoky environment, and t'nerefore may be ineffective under conditions of dense smoke. in order to eliminate this inconsistency, the Board believes that illumination levels should b2 specified in paragraph 812, which are consistent with the requirements of 14 CFR 25.811(c). Moreover, these and other accident experiences have shown that for various reasons aircraft emergency lighting systems often do not work or are proved ineffective in survivable accidents. Therefore, the Safety Board recommends that the Federal Aviation Administration:

> 4. Amend 14 CFR 25.812 to require exit sign brightness
>   and general illumination levels in the passenger
>   cabin that are consistent with those necessary to
>   provide adequate visibility in conditions of dense
>   smoke.

63

5. Amend 14 CFR 25.812 to provide an addition31 means for activating the main emergency lighting system to provide redundancy and thereby improve its reliability.

Emergency Evacuation Problems: A recurring problem of galley security was encountered in the UAL C-737 accident when, during impact, food and service items fell from the two aft cabin galley units. The impact, which was described by cabin attendants as a series of mild to moderate jolts acting forward and rearward, caused the four oven units and food carriers, the cold food trays, and the liquor supply units to be thrown to the floor near the rear service door. The Board previously has commented on the evacuation hazard caused by loose galley equipment and acknowledges a letter from the FAA dated February 16, 1973, which cites corrective actions to alleviate the galley security problem. Specifically, we are encouraged by recent amendments to Parts 25 and 121 of the Federal Aviation Regulations, which cover the retention of items of mass in passenger and crew compartments. Nevertheless we wish to reiterate our belief concerning the need for further improvements to ensure the security of galley equipment under crash landing loads. The Board is aware that an amendment to 14 CFR 25.789, which would require the installation of secondary retention devices on galley equipment, is under consideration for rulemaking action. In view of the steps that you have initiated to remedy this safety problem, the Safety Board is not making a formal recommendation at this time. However, we urge you to expedite your consideration of this matter in order that an amended galley retention regulation can be made effective at an early date.

This document will be released to the public on the date shown above. No public dissemination of this document should be made prior to that date.

Reed, Chairman, McAdams, Thayer, and Haley, Members, concurred in the above recommendations. Burgess, Member, was absent, not voting.

By John H. Reed
Chairman

CVR transcript Eastern Air Lines Flight 401 - 29 DEC 1972

Legenda

RDO - Radio transmission from accident aircraft
CAM - Cockpit Area Microphone sound or source
-1 - Voice identified as Captain
-2 - Voice identified as First Officer
-3 - Voice identified as Second Officer
TWR - Miami Controller (tower)

23.32:35	RDO-1	Miami Tower, Eastern 401 just turned on final
23.32:45	TWR	Who else called?
23.32:48	CAM-1	Go ahead and throw 'em out
23.32:52	RDO-1	Miami Tower, do you read, Eastern 401? Just turned on final
23.32:56	TWR	Eastern 401 Heavy, continue approach to 9 left
23.33:00	RDO-1	Coninue approach, roger
23.33:00	CAM-3	Continuous ignition. No smoke
	CAM-1	Coming on
	CAM-3	Brake system
	CAM-1	Okay
	CAM-3	Radar
	CAM-1	Up, off
	CAM-3	Hydraulic panels checked
	CAM-2	Thirty-five, thirty three
	CAM-1	Bert, is that handle in?
	CAM-?	* * *
	CAM-3	Engine crossbleeds are open

23.33:22 CAM-? Gear down

CAM-? * * *

CAM-1 I gotta

CAM-? .....

23.33:25 CAM-1 I gotta raise it back up

23.33:47 CAM-1 Now I'm gonna try it down one more time

CAM-2 All right

23.33:58 CAM [sound of altitude alert horn]

CAM-2 (Right) gear.

CAM-2 Well, want to tell 'em we'll take it around and circle around and # around?

23.34:05 RDO-1 Well ah, tower, this is Eastern, ah, 401. It looks like we're gonna have to circle, we don't have a light on our nose gear yet

23.34:14 TWR Eastern 401 heavy, roger, pull up, climb straight ahead to two thousand, go back to approach control, one twenty eight six

23.34:19 CAM-2 Twenty-two degrees.

CAM-2 Twenty-two degrees, gear up

CAM-1 Put power on it first, Bert. Thata boy.

CAM-1 Leave the # # gear down tll we fid out what we got

CAM-2 Allright

CAM-3 You want me to test the lights or not?

CAM-1 Yeah.

CAM-? * * seat back

CAM-1 Check it

CAM-2 Uh, Bob, it might be the light. Could you jiggle tha, the light?

	CAM-3	It's gotta, gotta come out a little bit and then snap in
	CAM-?	* *
	CAM-?	I'll put 'em on
23.34:21	RDO-1	Okay, going up to two thousand, one twenty-eight six
23.34:58	CAM-2	We're up to two thousand
	CAM-2	You want me to fly it, Bob?
	CAM-1	What frequency did he want us on, Bert?
	CAM-2	One twenty-eight six
	CAM-1	I'll talk to 'em
	CAM-3	It"s right ....
	CAM-1	Yeah, ...
	CAM-3	I can't make it pull out, either
	CAM-1	We got pressure
	CAM-3	Yes sir, all systems
	CAM-1	# #
23.35:09	RDO-1	All right ahh, Approach Control, Eastern 401, we're right over the airport here and climbing to two thousand feet. in fact, we've just
23.35:20	APP	Eastern 401, roger. Turn left heading three six zero and maintain two thousand, vectors to 9 Left final
23.35:28	RDO-1	Left three six zero
23.36:04	CAM-1	Put the ... on autopilot here
	CAM-2	Allright

CAM-1	See if you can get that light out	
	CAM-2	Allright
	CAM-1	Now push the switches just a ... forward.
	CAM-1	Okay.
	CAM-1	You got it sideways, then.
	CAM-?	Naw, I don't think it'll fit.
	CAM-1	You gotta turn it one quarter turn to the left.
23.36:27	APP	Eastern 401, turn left heading three zero zero
	RDO-1	Okay.
23.36:37	RDO-1	Three zero zero, Eastern 401
23.37:08	CAM-1	Hey, hey, get down there and see if that damn nose wheel's down. You better do that.
	CAM-2	You got a handkerchief or something so I can get a little better grip on this? Anything I can do with it?
	CAM-1	Get down there and see if that, see if that # thing ...
	CAM-2	This won't come out, Bob. If I had a pair of pliers, I could cushion it with that Kleenex
	CAM-3	I can give you pliers but if you force it, you'll break it, just believe me
	CAM-2	Yeah, I'll cushion it with Kleenex
	CAM-3	Oh, we can give you pliers
23.37:48	APP	Eastern, uh, 401 turn left heading two seven zero
23.37:53	RDO-1	Left two seven zero, roger

23.38:34 CAM-1 To # with it, to # with this. Go down ans see if it's lined up with the red line. That's all we care. # around with that # twenty-cent piec

CAM * * *

23.38:46 RDO-1 Eastern 401 'll go ah, out west just a little further if we can here and, ah, see if we can get this light to come on here

23.38:54 APP Allright, ah, we got you headed westbound there now, Eastern 401

23.38:56 RDO-1 Allright

CAM-1 How much fuel we got left on this # # # #

CAM-? Fifty two five

CAM-2 (It won't come out) no way

23.39:37 CAM-1 Did you ever take it out of there?

CAM-2 Huh?

CAM-1 Have you evre taken it out of there?

CAM-2 Hadn't till now

CAM-1 Put it in the wrong way, huh?

CAM-2 In there looks * square to me

CAM-? Can't you get the hole lined up?

CAM-? * * *

CAM-? Whatever's wrong?

CAM-1 (What's that?)

23.40:05 CAM-2 I think that's over the training field

CAM-? West heading you wanna go left or *

CAM-2 Naw that's right, we're about to cross Krome Avenue right now

23.40:17 CAM [Sound of click]

CAM-2	I don't know what the # holding that # # # # in	
	CAM-2	Always something, we coulda make schedule
23.40:38	CAM	[Sound of altitude alert]
	CAM-1	We can tell if that # # # # is down by looking down at our indices
	CAM-1	I'm sure it's down, there's no way it couldnt help but be
	CAM-2	I'm sure it is
	CAM-1	It freefalls down
	CAM-2	The tests didn't show that the lights worked anyway
	CAM-1	That 's right
	CAM-2	It's a faulty light
23.41:05	CAM-2	Bob, this # # # # just won't come out
	CAM-1	Allright leave it there
	CAM-3	I don't see it down there
	CAM-1	Huh?
	CAM-3	I don't see it
	CAM-1	You can't see that indis ... for the nosewheel ah, there's a place in there you can look and see if they're lined up
	CAM-3	I know, a little like a telescope
	CAM-1	Yeah
	CAM-3	Well...
	CAM-1	It's not lined up?

	CAM-3	I can't see it, it's pitch dark and I throw the little light I get ah nothing
23.41:31	CAM-4	Wheel-well lights on?
	CAM-3	Pardon?
	CAM-4	Wheel-well lights on?
	CAM-3	Yeah wheel well lights always on if the gear's down
	CAM-1	Now try it
23.41:40	APP	Eastern, ah 401 how are things comin' along out there?
23.41:44	RDO-1	Okay, we'd like to turn around and come, come back in
	CAM-1	Clear on left?
	CAM-2	Okay
23.41:47	APP	Eastern 401 turn left heading one eight zero
23.41:50	CAM-1	Huh?
23.41:51	RDO-1	One eighty
23.42:05	CAM-2	We did something to the altitude
	CAM-1	What?
23.42:07	CAM-2	We're still at two thousand right?
23.42:09	CAM-1	Hey, what's happening here?
	CAM	[Sound of click]
23.42:10	CAM	[Sound of six beeps similar to radio altimeter increasing in rate]
23.42:12		[Sound of impact]

The Ghosts of Flight 401

There are few air crashes that attracted so much interest as Eastern Airlines flight 401. Nobody really knows how it started, it was suddenly everywhere. Over the following months and years, employees of Eastern Air Lines began reporting sightings of the dead crew members, captain Robert Loft and second officer (flight engineer) Donald Repo, sitting on board other L-1011 (N318EA) flights. The story was that parts of Flight 401 were salvaged after the crash investigation and refitted into other L-1011s. The reported hauntings were only seen on the planes that used the spare parts. (Even though some parts were salvaged and re-used to maintain other airplanes in Eastern's fleet, the accident resulted in the total hull loss of N310EA and it was written off.) Sightings of the spirits of Don Repo and Bob Loft spread throughout Eastern Air Lines to the point where Eastern's management warned employees that they could face dismissal if caught spreading ghost stories.

Encounters with Repo's Ghost. Repo was a hands-on type of apparition. He was very concerned with safety. He appeared to a captain and told him there would never be another crash. They wouldn't let it happen. A woman was sitting next to an Eastern Airlines pilot who looked ill. She called a stewardess. The man disappeared before her and others. She identified Repo from a photograph. Another woman summoned a stewardess because she was concerned about the unresponsive man in an Eastern Airlines uniform in the seat next to her. The man disappeared in front of both of them and several other passengers. He was Repo. A stewardess saw a man in a flight engineer's uniform fixing an oven. The plane's flight engineer insisted he hadn't repaired it. When she saw Repo's picture, she recognized him. tewardess Faye Merryweather saw Repo's face looking out at her from an oven in the galley. She fetched two co-workers, one of whom had been a friend of Repo's. He recognized him. All three heard Repo warn them to watch for fire. Later, the airplane had serious engine problems and the last leg of the flight was canceled. It was learned that the galley had been salvaged from Flight 401. A flight engineer was mid-way through performing the routine pre-flight inspection when Repo appeared to him and told him he'd already done the job.

Repo and the Birds' Tribute. Don loved birds. When he was home in the morning, he'd drink his coffee in the screened-in patio and watch the birds at the feeder. His wife left the door slightly ajar so the dogs could enter or go out. Occasionally, a bird would fly in. Don's wife had to shoo it out with a broom. No bird had flown out without her help. On the day Don died, at least thirty birds appeared in the patio, flew back and forth, then flew out by themselves. He died about the time the birds said "farewell."

Captain Loft's Ghost's Appearances. Loft's ghost was seen on various flights, usually in first class or in the cockpit. He seemed to be content to appear, then vanish. A stewardess confronted Loft, asking him why he was on the plane. He wasn't on the passenger list. She reported this to the Captain who walked back with her. He recognized Loft who vanished in front of a dozen witnesses. A Captain and two flight attendants claimed to have seen and spoken to Loft before take-off and watched him vanish. One of the vice-presidents of Eastern Airlines spoke to a uniformed captain sitting in first class. Suddenly, he recognized Loft, at which time the apparition vanished.

Flight 401 Ghosts – Final Outcome. Many witnesses were credible. Conclusion was that the apparitions were real. The Federal Aviation Agency has records that fire broke out on the airplane that had Repo concerned. Eastern Airlines was somewhat skeptical of employees who reported ghostly experiences and suggested they seek psychological counseling at the company's expense. Although the airline refused to cooperate with paranormal investigators, it removed all of the Flight 401 salvaged parts from their aircraft. Over time, the reporting of ghost sightings stopped.

The story of the crash and its aftermath was documented first in John G. Fuller's 1976 book *The Ghost of Flight 401,* and later in Rob and Sarah Elder's 1977 book, *Crash.*

But that was not enough, soon two made-for-television movies based on the crash were aired in 1978:*Crash of Flight 401*, aired in October, was based on the Elders' book, and dramatized the crash, rescue efforts and NTSB investigation; while *The Ghost of Flight 401,* aired earlier in February, was based on Fuller's book and focuses more on the ghost sightings surrounding the aftermath.

Eastern Air Lines CEO Frank Borman called the ghost stories surrounding the crash "garbage". Eastern considered suing for libel, based on assertions of a cover-up by Eastern executives, but Borman opted not to, feeling a lawsuit would merely provide more publicity for the book. Loft's widow and children did sue Fuller, for infringement of Loft's right of publicity, for invasion of privacy, and for intentional infliction of emotional distress; but the lawsuit was dismissed and the dismissal upheld by the Florida Fourth District Court of Appeal.

The crash also appeared in a Season 5 episode of *Mayday* (also known as *Air Crash Investigation*). The episode was titled "Who's at the Controls?" (In some countries, the title "Fatal Distraction" was used.)

The flight was also mentioned in Season 1 episode 4 (entitled Phantom Traveler) of the television show *Supernatural.* This haunting became known all over the world as *"The Ghost of Flight 401."*

Other Air Crash Investigations

AIR CRASH INVESTIGATIONS

POLISH PRESIDENT DIES IN AIR CRASH

The Crash of Polish Air Force Flight 101

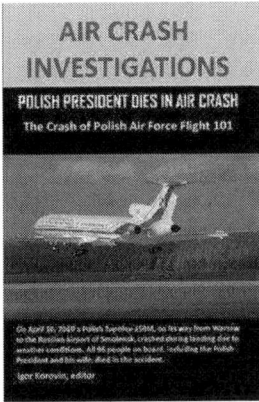

On April 10, 2010 a Polish Tupolev-154M, on its way from Warsaw to the Russian Airport of Smolensk, crashed during landing due to weather conditions. All 96 people on board, including the Polish President and his wife, died in the accident.

Igor Korovin, editor

On April 10, 2010 at 10:41 local time, approaching Runway 26 of Smolensk "Severny" airdrome, a Tupolev-154M aircraft of the State Aviation of the Republic of Poland crashed while conducting a non-regular international flight PLF 101 carrying passengers from Warsaw to Smolensk. The cause of the accident was the failure of the crew to take a timely decision to proceed to an alternate airdrome due to weather conditions at the airport of destination. All 96 persons on board, including Polish President Lech Kaczyński and his wife, died in the crash.

AIR CRASH INVESTIGATIONS

MASS MURDER IN THE SKY

The Bombing of Air India Flight 182

Air India Flight 182 a Boeing 747-237B was blown up by a bomb on June 23, 1985, and crashed into the Atlantic Ocean near the coast of Ireland, killing 329 people. Investigation and prosecution took almost 25 years. The main suspects in the bombing were members of the Sikh separatist Babbar Khalsa.

Alistair Fitzgerald, editor

On 23 June 1985, Air India Flight 182, a Boeing 747-237B was on its way from Montreal, Canada, to London when it was blown up while in Irish airspace, and crashed into the Atlantic Ocean. 329 people perished. It was the largest mass murder in modern Canadian history. The explosion and downing of the carrier was related to the Narita Airport Bombing. Investigation and prosecution took 25 years. The suspects were members of the Sikh separatist Babbar Khalsa. Inderjit Singh Reyat, the only person convicted, was sentenced to 15 years in prison.

AIR CRASH INVESTIGATIONS

THE END OF THE CONCORDE ERA

The Crash of Air France Flight 4590

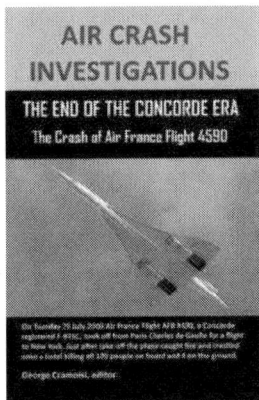

On Tuesday 25 July 2000 Air France Flight AFR 4590, a Concorde registered F-BTSC, took off from Paris Charles de Gaulle for a flight to New York. Just after take off the plane caught fire and crashed onto a hotel killing all 109 people on board and 4 on the ground.

George Cramoisi, editor

On Tuesday 25 July 2000 Air France Flight AFR 4590, a Concorde registered F-BTSC, took off from Paris Charles de Gaulle, to undertake a charter flight to New York with nine crew members and one hundred passengers on board. During takeoff from runway 26 right at Roissy Charles de Gaulle Airport, a tyre was damaged. A major fire broke out. The aircraft was unable to gain height or speed and crashed onto a hotel, killing all 109 people on board and 4 on the ground. The crash would become the end of the Concorde era.

AIR CRASH INVESTIGATIONS

LOCKERBIE

The Bombing of PANAM Flight 103

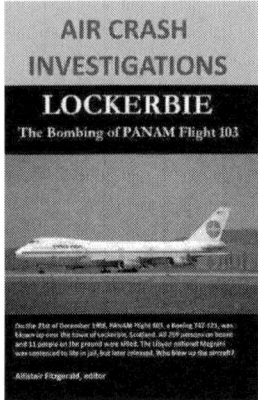

On the 21st of December 1988, PANAM Flight 103, a Boeing 747-121, on its way from London Heathrow to New York, was blown up over the town of Lockerbie, Scotland. All 259 persons on board of the aircraft and 11 residents of the town of Lockerbie were killed. In 2001 the Libyan Megrahi was sentenced to life imprisonment in Scotland. In 2009 Megrahi applied to be released from jail on compassionate grounds. His appeal was granted and on the 20th of August 2009 he was released from prison. But was Megrahi really guilty?

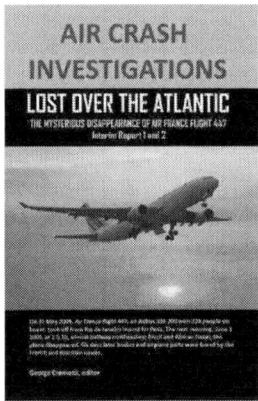

AIR CRASH INVESTIGATIONS

LOST OVER THE ATLANTIC

THE MYSTERIOUS DISAPPEARANCE OF AIR FRANCE FLIGHT 447
Interim Report 1 and 2

On 31 May 2009, flight AF447, an Airbus A330-200, took off from Rio de Janeiro bound for Paris. At 2 h 10, a position message and some maintenance messages were transmitted by the ACARS automatic system. After this nothing was heard of from the aircraft. Six days later bodies and airplane parts were found by the French and Brazilian navies. All 228 passengers and crew members on board are presumed to have perished in the accident. A massive search by air and sea craft for the plane's black boxes failed so far.

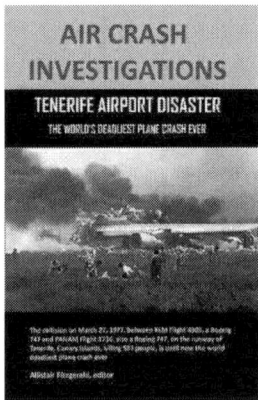

AIR CRASH INVESTIGATIONS

TENERIFE AIRPORT DISASTER

THE WORLD'S DEADLIEST PLANE CRASH EVER

On Sunday, March 27, 1977 KLM Flight 4805 and PANAM Flight 1736 both approached Las Palmas Airport in the Canary Islands, when a terrorist's bomb exploded on the airport. Both flights were diverted to the neighboring island of Tenerife. After Las Palmas Airport reopened first KLM Flight 4805 was cleared for takeoff, a few minutes later PANAM 1736 was cleared. Due to a number of misunderstandings both aircraft collided on the runway of Tenerife Airport during takeoff, killing 583 people.

AIR CRASH INVESTIGATIONS

THE PLANE THAT VANISHED

The Crash of Adam Air Flight 574

On 1 January 2007, a Boeing 737-4Q8, operated by Adam Air as flight DHI 574, was on a flight from Surabaya, East Java to Manado, Sulawesi, in Indonesia, when it suddenly vanished from radar. There were 102 people on board.

George Cramoisi, Editor

On 1 January 2007, a Boeing 737-4Q8, operated by Adam Air as flight DHI 574, was on a flight from Surabaya, East Java to Manado, Sulawesi, at FL 350 (35,000 feet) when it suddenly disappeared from radar. There were 102 people on board.. Nine days later wreckage was found floating in the sea near the island of Sulawesi. The black boxes revealed that the pilots were so engrossed in trouble shooting the IRS that they forgot to fly the plane, resulting in the crash that cost the lives of all aboard.

AIR CRASH INVESTIGATIONS

PILOT ERROR KILLS 50 PEOPLE IN BUFFALO

The Crash of Colgan Air Flight 3407

Colgan Air Flight 3407, a Bombardier DHC-8-400, crashed 5 nautical miles before the international airport of Buffalo, New York, because of the captain's failure to manage the flight, killing all 49 people on board and one on the ground

Allistair Fitzgerald, editor

On February 12, 2009, about 2217 eastern standard time, Colgan Air, Flight 3407, a Bombardier DHC-8-400, on approach to Buffalo-Niagara International Airport, crashed into a residence in Clarence Center, New York, 5 nautical miles northeast of the airport. The 2 pilots, 2 flight attendants, and 45 passengers aboard the airplane were killed, one person on the ground was killed, and the airplane was destroyed. The National Transportation Safety Board determined that the probable cause of this accident was a pilot's error.

AIR CRASH INVESTIGATIONS

HARD LANDING KILLS 9

The Crash of Turkish Airlines Flight TK 1951 on Amsterdam Schiphol Airport

On 25 February 2009, Turkish Airlines flight 1951, a Boeing 737-800, with 135 people on board, was on its way from Istanbul in Turkey to Amsterdam Schiphol Airport in the Netherlands. Due to a malfunctioning radio altimeter and a failure to implement proper stall recovery procedure the plane stalled and crashed just short of the runway of Schiphol Airport, killing 9 and injuring 135 people.

Igor Korsico, editor

On 25 February 2009 a Boeing 737-800, flight TK1951, operated by Turkish Airlines was flying from Istanbul in Turkey to Amsterdam Schiphol Airport. There were 135 people on board. During the approach to the runway at Schiphol airport, the aircraft crashed about 1.5 kilometres from the threshold of the runway. This accident cost the lives of four crew members, and five passengers, 120 people sustained injuries. The crash was caused by a malfunctioning radio altimeter and a failure to implement the stall recovery procedure correctly.

AIR CRASH INVESTIGATIONS

The Crash of American Airlines Flight 587

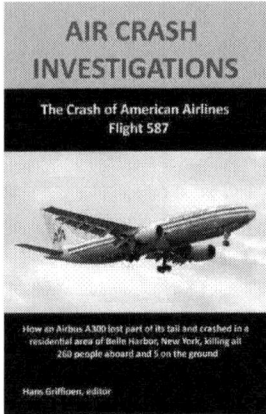

How an Airbus A300 lost part of its tail and crashed in a residential area of Belle Harbor, New York, killing all 260 people aboard and 5 on the ground

Hans Griffioen, editor

On November 12, 2001, American Airlines flight 587, an Airbus A300-605R, took off from John F. Kennedy International Airport, New York. Flight 587 was a scheduled passenger flight to Santo Domingo, Dominican Republic, with a crew of 9 and 251 passengers aboard the airplane. Shortly after take-off the airplane lost its tail, the engines subsequently separated in flight and the airplane crashed into a residential area of Belle Harbor, New York. All 260 people aboard the airplane and 5 people on the ground were killed, and the airplane was destroyed by impact forces and a post crash fire.

AIR CRASH INVESTIGATIONS

THE CRASH OF AIR FRANCE FLIGHT 358

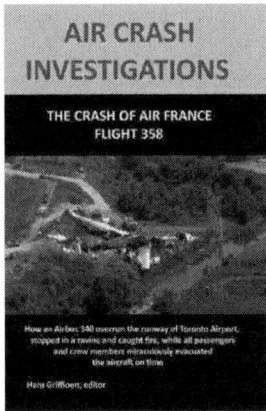

How an Airbus 340 overrun the runway of Toronto Airport, stopped in a ravine and caught fire, while all passengers and crew members miraculously evacuated the aircraft on time

Hans Griffioen, editor

On August 2, 2005 Air France Flight 358, an Airbus A340, departed Paris, on a flight to Toronto, Canada, with 297 passengers and 12 crew members on board. On final approach, the aircraft's weather radar was displaying heavy precipitation. The aircraft touched down 3800 feet down the runway, and was not able to stop before the end of it. The aircraft stopped in a ravine and caught fire. All passengers and crew members were able to evacuate the aircraft on time. Only 2 crew members and 10 passengers were seriously injured during the crash and the evacuation.

AIR CRASH INVESTIGATIONS

The Crash of Swissair Flight 111

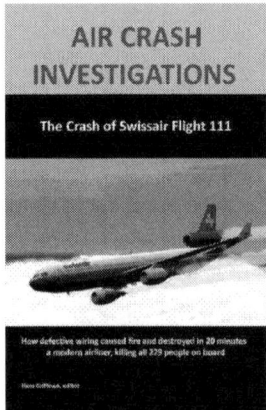

How defective wiring caused fire and destroyed in 20 minutes a modern airliner, killing all 229 people on board

Hans Griffioen, editor

On 2 September 1998, Swissair Flight SR 111 departed New York, flight to Geneva, Switzerland, with 215 passengers and 14 crew members on board. About 53 minutes after departure, the flight crew smelled an abnormal odour in the cockpit. They decided to divert to the Halifax International Airport. They were unaware that a fire was spreading above the ceiling in the front area of the aircraft. They did not make it to Halifax, 20 minutes later the aircraft crashed in the North Atlantic near Peggy's Cove, Nova Scotia, Canada. There were no survivors, 229 people died in the incident.

AIR CRASH INVESTIGATIONS

The Crash of Comair Flight 5191

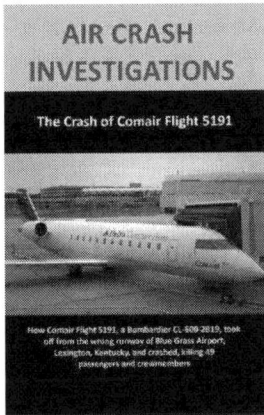

How Comair Flight 5191, a Bombardier CL-600-2B19, took off from the wrong runway of Blue Grass Airport, Lexington, Kentucky, and crashed, killing 49 passengers and crewmembers

On August 27, 2006, Comair Flight 5191, a Bombardier CL-600-2B19, crashed during takeoff from the wrong runway of Blue Grass Airport, Lexington, Kentucky, killing 49 of the 50 people aboard. From the beginning everything went wrong. First the captain and first officer boarded the wrong airplane, only after starting the auxiliary power unit they found out they were in the wrong aircraft. Taxiing to the takeoff position the captain and first officer were so engaged in a private conversation that they did not realize they took the wrong runway. The air traffic controller did not notice anything.

AIR CRASH INVESTIGATIONS

The Crash of Helios Airways Flight 522

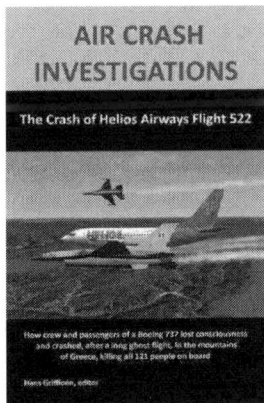

How crew and passengers of a Boeing 737 lost consciousness and crashed, after a long ghost flight, in the mountains of Greece, killing all 121 people on board

Hans Griffioen, editor

On 14 August 2005, a Boeing 737-300 aircraft departed from Larnaca, Cyprus, for Prague. As the aircraft climbed through 16.000 ft, the Captain contacted the company Operations Centre and reported a problem. Thereafter, there was no response to radio calls to the aircraft. At 07:21 h, the aircraft was intercepted by two F-16 aircraft of the Hellenic Air Force. They observed the aircraft and reported no external damage. The aircraft crashed approximately 33 km northwest of the Athens International Airport. All 121 people on board were killed.

AIR CRASH INVESTIGATIONS

The Crash of Aeroflot Flight 821

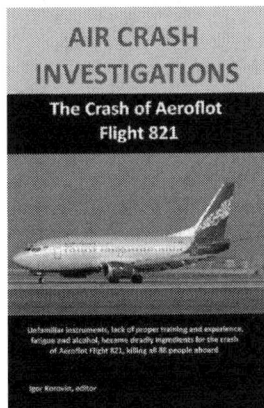

Unfamiliar instruments, lack of proper training and experience, fatigue and alcohol, became deadly ingredients for the crash of Aeroflot Flight 821, killing all 88 people aboard

Igor Konovio, editor

On 14 September 2008 Aeroflot Flight 821, a Boeing 737-505, operated by Aeroflot-Nord, a subsidiary of the Russian airline Aeroflot, crashed on approach to Bolshoye Savino Airport, Perm, Russia. All 82 passengers and 6 crew members were killed. The aircraft was completely destroyed. According to the final investigation report, the main reason of the crash was pilot error. Both pilots had lost spatial orientation, lack of proper training, insufficient knowledge of English and fatigue from lack of adequate rest. Alcohol in the Captain's blood may also have contributed to the accident.

AIR CRASH INVESTIGATIONS

The Crash of Alaska Airlines Flight 261

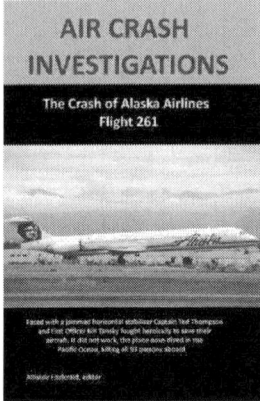

On January 31, 2000, Alaska Airlines, Flight 261, a McDonnell Douglas MD-83, was on its way from Puerto Vallarta, Mexico, to Seattle, Washington, when suddenly the horizontal stabilizer of the plane jammed. Captain Thompson and First officer Tansky tried to make an emergency landing in Los Angeles. The plane suddenly crashed into the Pacific Ocean, killing all 93 people aboard. The NTSB concluded that the crash was caused by insufficient maintenance. The crash of Alaska Airlines Flight 261 could have been avoided.

AIR CRASH INVESTIGATIONS

DISASTER IN THE EVERGLADES
The Crash of ValuJet Flight 592

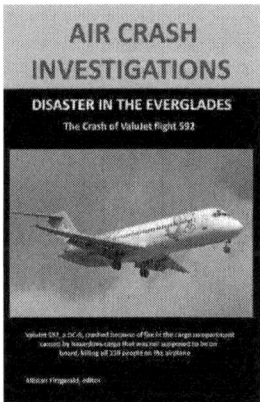

On May 11, 1996, at 1413:42 eastern daylight time, a Douglas DC-9-32 crashed into the Everglades 10 minutes after takeoff from Miami International Airport, Miami, Florida. The airplane was being operated by ValuJet Airlines, Inc., as flight 592 and was on its way to Atlanta, Georgia. Both pilots, the three flight attendants, and all 105 passengers were killed. The NTSB determined that the cause of the accident, was a fire in the airplane's cargo compartment, initiated by the actuation of an oxygen generator being improperly carried as cargo.

AIR CRASH INVESTIGATIONS

RUNNING OUT OF FUEL
How an Airbus 330 Managed to Fly 100 Miles without Fuel and Land Safely

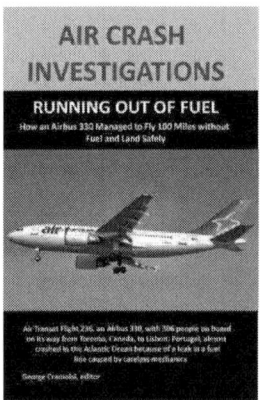

On August 24, 2001, Air Transat Flight 236, an Airbus 330, was on its way from Toronto, Canada to Lisbon, Portugal with 306 people on board. Above the Atlantic Ocean, the crew noticed a dangerous fuel imbalance. After flying 100 miles without fuel the crew managed to land the aircraft at the Lajes Airport at 06:45. Only 16 passengers and 2 cabin-crew members received injuries. The investigation uncovered a large crack in the fuel line of the right engine, caused by mistakes during an engine change just before the start of the flight.

83

AIR CRASH
INVESTIGATIONS
MECHANICAL FAILURE OR SUICIDE (1)
The Crash of SilkAir Flight 185

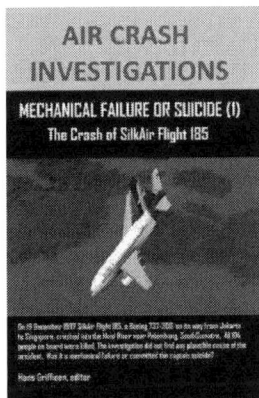

On 19 December 1997 SilkAir Flight 185, a Boeing 737-300, operated by SilkAir, Singapore, on its way from Jakarta to Singapore, crashed at about 16:13 local time into the Musi river near Palembang, South Sumatra. All 97 passengers and seven crew members were killed. Prior to the sudden descent from 35,000 feet, the flight data recorders suddenly stopped recording at different times. There were no mayday calls transmitted from the airplane prior or during the rapid descent. The weather at the time of the crash was fine.

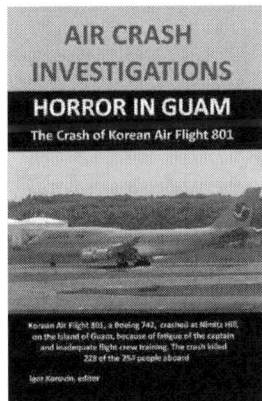

AIR CRASH
INVESTIGATIONS
HORROR IN GUAM
The Crash of Korean Air Flight 801

On August 6, 1997, about 0142:26 Guam local time, Korean Air flight 801, a Boeing 747-300, crashed at Nimitz Hill, Guam. The aircraft was on its way from Seoul, Korea to Guam with 237 passengers and a crew of 17 on board. Of the 254 persons on board, 228 were killed. The airplane was destroyed by impact forces and a post-crash fire. The National Transportation Safety Board determined that the probable cause of the accident was captain's fatigue and Korean Air's inadequate flight crew training.

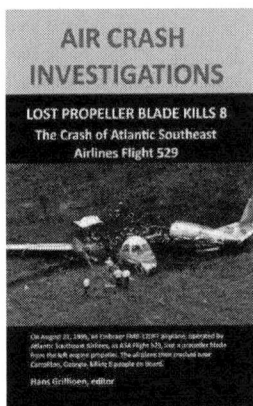

AIR CRASH
INVESTIGATIONS
LOST PROPELLER BLADE KILLS 8
The Crash of Atlantic Southeast
Airlines Flight 529

This book explains the accident involving Atlantic Southeast Airlines flight 529, an EMB-120RT airplane, which lost a propeller blade and crashed near Carrollton, Georgia, on August 21, 1995. The accident killed 8 people on board. Safety issues in the report focused on manufacturer engineering practices, propeller blade maintenance repair, propeller testing and inspection procedures, the relaying of emergency information by air traffic controllers, crew resource management training, and the design of crash axes carried in aircraft.

84

AIR CRASH
INVESTIGATIONS
SUDDENLY FALLING APART
The Crash of Lauda Air Flight NG 104

Lauda Air Flight NG 104, a Boeing 767-300 ER of Austrian nationality was on a scheduled passenger flight Hong Kong-Bangkok-Vienna, Austria. NG 104 departed Hong Kong Airport on May 26, 1991, and made an intermediate landing at Bangkok Airport. The flight departed Bangkok Airport at 1602 hours. The airplane disappeared from air traffic radar at 1617 hours, about 94 nautical miles northwest of Bangkok. The probable cause of this accident is attributed to an uncommanded in-flight deployment of the left engine thrust reverser. All 223 people on board died in the accident.

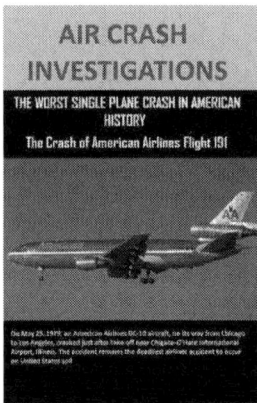

AIR CRASH
INVESTIGATIONS
THE WORST SINGLE PLANE CRASH IN AMERICAN HISTORY
The Crash of American Airlines Flight 191

On May 25, 1979, American Airlines Flight 191, a McDonnell-Douglas DC-10-10 aircraft, on its way from Chicago to Los Angeles, crashed just after take-off near Chicago-O'Hare International Airport, Illinois. During the take off the left engine and pylon assembly and about 3 ft of the leading edge of the left wing separated from the aircraft and fell to the runway. Flight 191 crashed killing two hundred and seventy one persons on board and two persons on the ground. The accident remains the deadliest airliner accident to occur on United States soil.

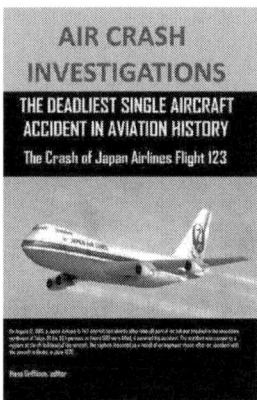

AIR CRASH
INVESTIGATIONS
THE DEADLIEST SINGLE AIRCRAFT ACCIDENT IN AVIATION HISTORY
The Crash of Japan Airlines Flight 123

On August 12, 1985, a Japan Airlines B-747 aircraft lost, shortly after take-off, part of its tail and crashed in the mountains northwest of Tokyo. Of the 524 persons on board 520 were killed, 4 survived the accident. The accident was caused by a rupture of the aft pressure bulkhead of the aircraft, and the subsequent ruptures of a part of the fuselage tail, vertical fin and hydraulic flight control systems. The rupture happened as the result of an improper repair after an accident with the aircraft in Osaka, in June 1978.

AIR CRASH INVESTIGATIONS

DRAMA IN SIOUX CITY

The Crash of United Airlines Flight 232

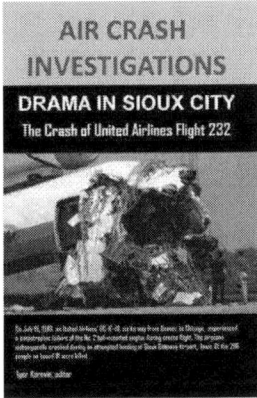

On July 19, 1989, an United Airlines' DC-10-10, on its way from Denver to Chicago, experienced a catastrophic failure of the No. 2 tail-mounted engine during cruise flight. The heroic pilots did all they could to bring the flight to a good end. But, notwithstanding all the attempts, the airplane subsequently crashed during an attempted landing at Sioux Gateway Airport, Iowa. Of the 296 people on board 111 were killed.

Igor Korovin, editor

AIR CRASH INVESTIGATIONS

JAMMED RUDDER KILLS 132

The Crash of USAir Flight 427

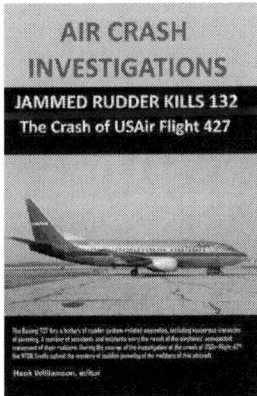

The Boeing 737 has a history of rudder system-related anomalies, including numerous instances of jamming. During the course of the four and a half year investigation of the crash of USAir Flight 427 near Aliquippa, Pennsylvania, killing 132 people, the NTSB discovered that the PCU's dual servo valve could jam as well as deflect the rudder in the opposite direction of the pilots' input, due to thermal shock, caused when cold PCUs are injected with hot hydraulic fluid. This finally solved the mystery of sudden jamming of the rudders of this aircraft.

Henk Williamson, editor

AIR CRASH INVESTIGATIONS

MYSTERIOUS CRASH KILLS 25

The Crash of United Airlines Flight 585

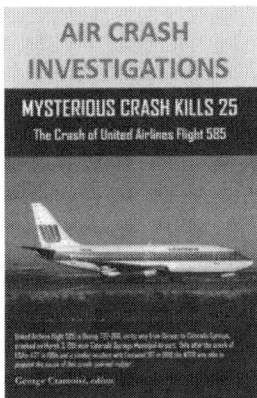

This amended report explains the accident involving United Airlines flight 585, a Boeing 737-200, on its way from Denver to Colorado Springs, which crashed on March 3, 1991 near Colorado Springs Municipal Airport. Only after the crash of USAir 427 in 1994 and a similar incident with Eastwind 517 in 1996 the NTSB was able to pinpoint the cause of this crash: jammed rudder. The Boeing 737 has a history of rudder system-related anomalies, this finally solved the mystery of sudden jamming of the rudders of this aircraft.

George Cramoisi, editor

AIR CRASH INVESTIGATIONS

MECHANICAL FAILURE OR SUICIDE (2)

The NTSB (USA) View of the Crash of EgyptAir Flight 990

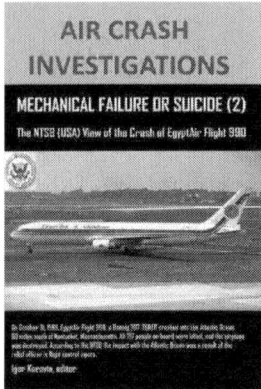

On October 31, 1999, EgyptAir Flight 990, a Boeing 767-366ER crashed into the Atlantic Ocean 60 miles south of Nantucket, Massachusetts. All 217 people on board were killed, and the airplane was destroyed. According to the NTSB, the impact with the Atlantic Ocean was a result of the relief officer's flight control inputs.

Igor Korovin, editor

On October 31, 1999, EgyptAir flight 990, a Boeing 767-366ER crashed into the Atlantic Ocean 60 miles south of Nantucket, Massachusetts. All 217 people on board were killed, and the airplane was destroyed. The US National Transportation Safety Board determines that the probable cause of the accident is the airplane's departure from normal cruise flight and subsequent impact with the Atlantic Ocean as a result of the relief first officer's flight control inputs. The reason for the relief first officer's actions was not determined.

AIR CRASH INVESTIGATIONS

MECHANICAL FAILURE OR SUICIDE (3)

The E.C.A.A. (Egypt) View of the Crash of EgyptAir Flight 990

On October 31, 1999, EgyptAir Flight 990, a Boeing 767-366ER crashed into the Atlantic Ocean 60 miles south of Nantucket, Massachusetts. All 217 people on board were killed, and the airplane was destroyed. According to the Egyptian Investigation Team a mechanical defect is the most likely cause of the accident.

Igor Korovin, editor

On October 31, 1999, EgyptAir flight 990, a Boeing 767-366ER crashed into the Atlantic Ocean 60 miles south of Nantucket, Massachusetts. All 217 people on board were killed, and the airplane was destroyed. Contrary to the conclusions of the American NTSB the Egyptian Investigation Team concludes that a mechanical defect is the most likely cause of the accident. According to the Egyptians there is no evidence to support a conclusion that the First Officer intentionally dove the airplane into the ocean in fact.

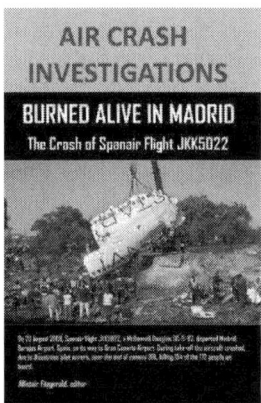

AIR CRASH INVESTIGATIONS

BURNED ALIVE IN MADRID

The Crash of Spanair Flight JKK5022

On 20 August 2008, Spanair Flight JKK5022, a McDonnell Douglas DC-9-82 departed Madrid Barajas Airport. Spain, on its way to Gran Canaria Airport. During take-off the aircraft crashed, due to disastrous pilot errors, soon the end of runway 36L, killing 154 of the 172 people on board.

Alistair Fitzgerald, editor

On 20 August 2008, Spanair flight JKK5022, a McDonnell Douglas DC-9-82 (MD-82), crashed during take-off from Barajas Airport in Madrid, The investigation revealed that the accident occurred as the aircraft attempted to take off, because the pilots had omitted to deploy the flaps and slats ready for take-off. The MD-82 warning system, that should have alerted the pilots that the plane was incorrectly configured for take-off, did not sound a warning. Of the 172 people on board 154 perished in the accident. Most burned alive.

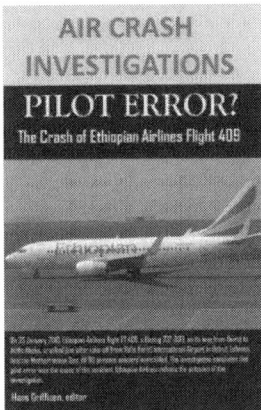

On 25 January 2010, at 00:41:30 UTC, Ethiopian Airlines flight ET 409, a Boeing 737-800, on its way from Beirut to Addis Abeba, crashed just after take-off from Rafic Hariri International Airport in Beirut, Lebanon, into the Mediterranean Sea about 5 NM South West of Beirut International Airport. All 90 persons onboard were killed in the accident. The investigation concluded that the probable causes of the accident were pilot errors due to loss of situational awareness. Ethiopian Airlines refutes this conclusion.

On 4 October 1992, El Al Israel Airlines Flight 1862, a Boeing 747-200 Freighter, departed from Schiphol Airport, Amsterdam, on its way to Tel Aviv, Israel. Seven minutes after take-off the plane lost engine no. 3 and 4 and crashed in an apartment block just outside Amsterdam, killing 43 people (4 crewmembers and 39 on the ground). The investigation concluded that the design and certification of the B 747 pylon was inadequate to provide the required level of safety. Furthermore the system to ensure structural integrity by inspection failed.

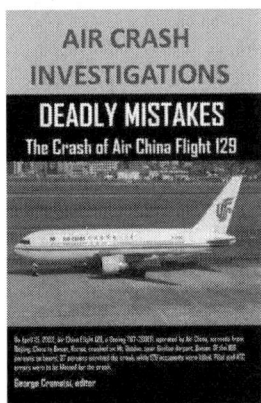

On April 15, 2002, about 11:21:17, Air China flight 129, a Boeing 767-200ER, operated by Air China, en route from Beijing, China to Busan, Korea, crashed on Mt. Dotdae, near Gimhae Airport, Busan. Of the 166 persons on board, 37 persons survived the crash, while 129 occupants were killed. The probable cause of the crash was pilot and ATC errors, while the airport did not inform the captain of the bad weather conditions at the time of landing in Busan. Because of these conditions eight previous flights were diverted to other airports.

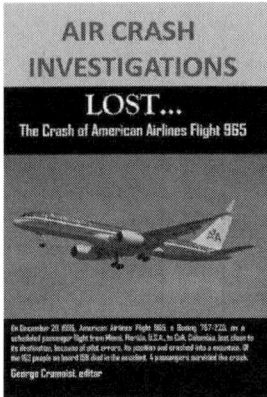

On December 20, 1995, American Airlines Flight 965, a Boeing 757-223, was on a scheduled passenger flight from Miami, Florida, U.S.A., to Cali, Colombia. Close to its final destination the pilots erroneously cleared the approach waypoints from their navigation computer. When the controller asked the pilots to check back in over Tuluá, north of Cali, it was no longer programmed into the computer. They were lost and the aircraft crashed into a mountain. Of the 163 people on board, 4 passengers survived the accident.

On 25 December 2003, Union des Transport Aériens de Guinée Flight GIH 141, a Boeing 727-223, on a flight from Conakry (Guinea) to Kufra (Libya), Beirut (Lebanon) and Dubai (United Arab Emirates) stopped over at Cotonou, Republic of Benin. During takeoff the airplane, overloaded in an anarchic manner, was not able to climb properly and struck an airport building on the extended runway centerline, and crashed onto the beach, killing 151 of the 163 people on board. The crew was unknown with the forward center of gravity of the aircraft.

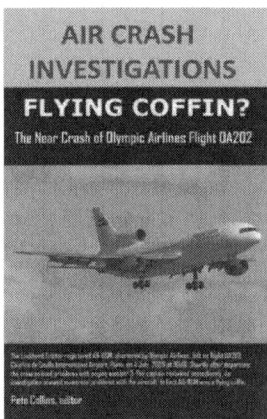

The Lockheed 1011 registered A6-BSM, chartered by Olympic Airlines, left as flight OA202 Charles de Gaulle International Airport, Paris, on 4 July 2005 at 16h18. Shortly after departure there were engine problems. The captain returned immediately. An investigation by the French BEA showed numerous technical problems with the aircraft, such as fuel and hydraulic leakages, non-working fire alarms and lack of maintenance. The flight crew was not properly licensed and the insurance was insufficient. In fact A6-BSM was a flying coffin.

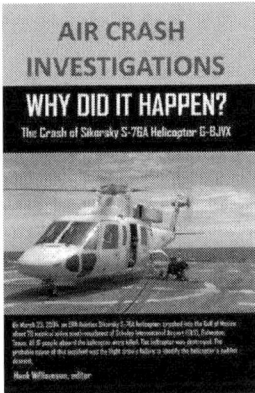

On March 23, 2004, about 1918:34 central standard time, an Era Aviation Sikorsky S-76 helicopter, crashed into the Gulf of Mexico about 70 nautical miles south-southeast of Scholes International Airport (GLS), Galveston, Texas. The helicopter was en route to the drilling ship Discoverer Spirit. All 10 people aboard the helicopter were killed. The helicopter was destroyed. The probable cause of this accident was the flight crew's failure to identify and arrest the helicopter's descent which resulted in controlled flight into terrain.

During the night of 04th May 2007, the B737-800, registration 5Y-KYA, operated by Kenya Airways as flight KQA 507 from Abidjan international airport (Ivory Coast), to the Jomo Kenyatta airport Nairobi (Kenya), made a scheduled stop-over at the Douala international airport (Cameroon). Shortly after take-off at about 1000 ft, the aircraft entered into a slow right roll that increased continuously and eventually ended up in a spiral dive, the airplane crashed in a mangrove swamp, killing all 114 people aboard. The captain, as pilot flying, lost complete control.

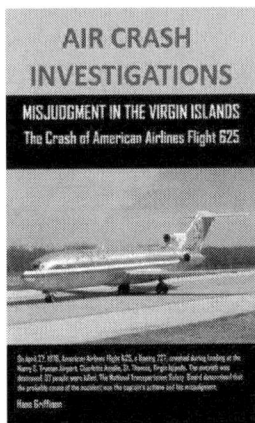

On April 27, 1976, American Airlines Flight 625, a Boeing 727, during landing at the Harry S Truman Airport, Charlotte Amalie, St. Thomas, Virgin Islands, overran the end of runway 9, struck the ILS antenna, crashed through a fence, and hit a building located about 1,040 feet beyond the departure end of the runway. The aircraft was destroyed, 35 passengers and 2 flight attendants were killed. The National Transportation Safety Board determined that the probable cause of the accident was the captain's actions and his misjudgment during landing.

AIR CRASH
INVESTIGATIONS
LOST OVER THE ATLANTIC
The Crash of Air France Flight 447
THE FINAL REPORT

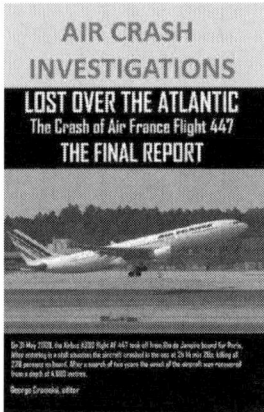

On 31 May 2009, the Airbus A330 flight AF 447 took off from Rio de Janeiro Galeão airport bound for Paris Charles de Gaulle. At 2h 10min 05, likely following the obstruction of the Pitot probes by ice crystals, the speed indications became incorrect and some automatic systems disconnected, the aeroplane came in a stall situation and crashed in the sea at 2 h 14 min 28s, killing all 228 persons on board. It took two years to recover the wreck of the aircraft from a depth of 4.000 metres. After two intermediate reports this is the final report of the crash.

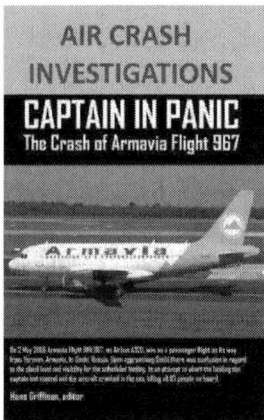

AIR CRASH
INVESTIGATIONS
CAPTAIN IN PANIC
The Crash of Armavia Flight 967

On 2 May 2006 Armavia Flight RNV 967, an Airbus A320, was as a passenger flight on its way from Yerevan, Armenia to Sochi, Russia. Upon approaching Sochi there was confusion in regard to the cloud level and visibility for the scheduled landing. While trying to land the air traffic control ordered the captain to abort the landing. In the attempt to abort the captain lost control and the aircraft crashed in the sea, killing all 113 people on board. Contributing factors were not maintaining strict cockpit rules and deficiencies by air traffic control.

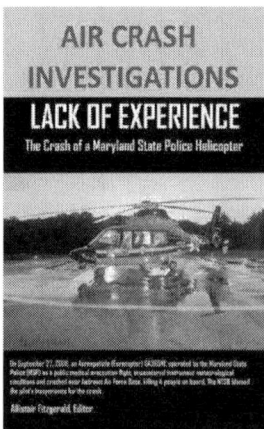

AIR CRASH
INVESTIGATIONS
LACK OF EXPERIENCE
The Crash of a Maryland State Police Helicopter

On September 27, 2008, an Aerospatiale (Eurocopter) SA365N1, call sign Trooper 2, operated by the Maryland State Police (MSP) as a public medical evacuation flight, encountered b ad weather en route to the hospital and was diverted to Andrews Air Force Base (ADW), Camp Springs, Maryland, 3.2 miles north of the runway 19R threshold at ADW, the helicopter impacted terrain and crashed. The commercial pilot, one flight paramedic, one field provider, and one automobile accident patients being transported were killed. The NTSB blamed the pilot's inexperience for the crash.

AIR CRASH INVESTIGATIONS

FATIGUE?

The Crash of Federal Express Flight 1478

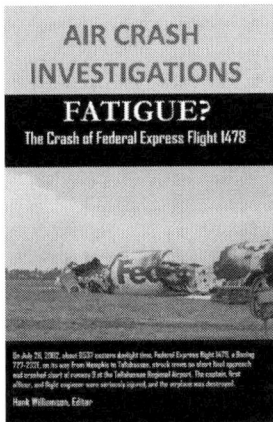

On July 26, 2002, about 0537 eastern daylight time, Federal Express flight 1478, a Boeing 727-232F, on its way from Memphis International Airport to Tallahassee Regional airport, struck trees on short final approach and crashed short of runway 9 at the Tallahassee Regional Airport, Florida. The captain, first officer, and flight engineer were seriously injured, and the airplane was destroyed. The National Transportation Safety Board determines that the probable cause of the accident was the crew's failure to establish and maintain a proper glidepath during the approach to landing.

AIR CRASH INVESTIGATIONS

FAILING BRAKES

The Crash of TAM Linhas Aereas Flight 3054

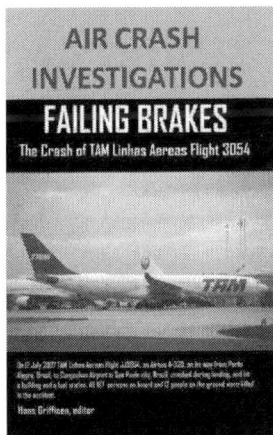

On 17 July 2007 an Airbus A-320, operated as flight JJ3054 by the Brazilian company TAM Linhas Aéreas, was on its way from Porto Alegre, Brazil, for a domestic flight to Congonhas Airport in São Paulo city, Brazil. During the landing, the aircraft was not slowing down as expected, veered to the left, overran the left edge of the runway, crossed over the Washington Luís Avenue, and collided with a building, and with a fuel service station. All 187 persons on board and 12 people on the ground were killed in the accident.

AIR CRASH INVESTIGATIONS

IN-FLIGHT ENGINE FAILURE

The Crash of Air Algerie Flight 6289

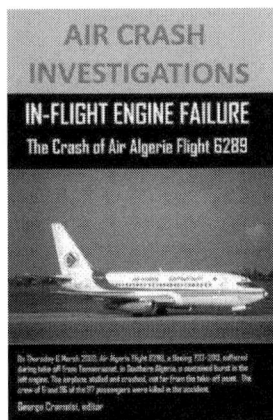

On Thursday 6 March 2003, Air Algérie Flight DAH 6289, a Boeing 737-200, suffered during take-off from Tamanrasset, in Southern Algeria, a contained burst in the left engine. The airplane swung to the left, lost speed progressively, stalled and crashed, with the landing gear still extended, about one thousand six hundred and forty-five meters from the takeoff point, to the left of the runway extended centerline. The crew and 96 passengers were killed in the accident, one passenger survived. The airplane was on a domestic flight from Tamanrasset to Ghardaïa and Algiers.

AIR CRASH INVESTIGATIONS

EYE OF THE NEEDLE

The Crash of British Airways Flight 38

On 28 November 2008, a Boeing 777-200ER, operated by British Airways as flight BA38, on its way from Beijing, China, to London (Heathrow), suffered on approach to Heathrow Airport an in-flight engine rollback. At 720 feet agl, both engines ceased responding to autothrottle commands. The result was that the aircraft touched down 330 m short of the paved surface of Runway 27L at London Heathrow. The reduction in thrust was due to restricted fuel flow to both engines, caused by the forming of ice in the fuel system. The aircraft was destroyed, but there were no casualties.

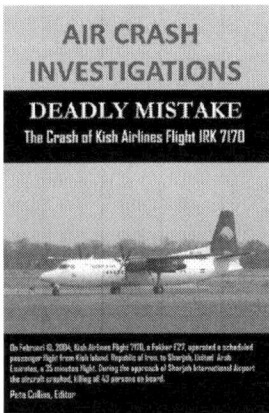

AIR CRASH INVESTIGATIONS

DEADLY MISTAKE

The Crash of Kish Airlines Flight IRK 7170

On February 10, 2004, Kish Airlines Flight IRK 7170, a Fokker F27, operated a scheduled passenger flight from Kish Island, Islamic Republic of Iran, to Sharjah, United Arab Emirates, a 35 minutes flight. During the approach of Sharjah International Airport, the aircraft was observed to pitch down and suddenly turn to the left. The aircraft continued to descend and turn at high pitch and roll angles and impacted a sandy area 2.6 nm from the runway threshold. A large explosion was seen. The aircraft was destroyed and there were 43 fatalities.

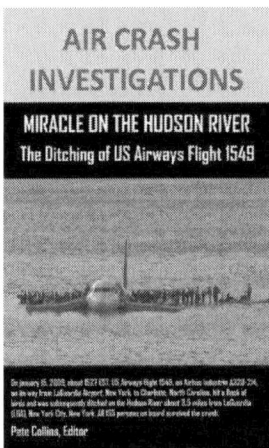

AIR CRASH INVESTIGATIONS

MIRACLE ON THE HUDSON RIVER

The Ditching of US Airways Flight 1549

On January 15, 2009, about 1527 eastern standard time, US Airways flight 1549, an Airbus Industrie A320-214, experienced an almost complete loss of thrust in both engines after encountering a flock of birds and was subsequently ditched on the Hudson River about 8.5 miles from LaGuardia Airport (LGA), New York City, New York. The flight was en route to Charlotte Douglas International Airport, Charlotte, North Carolina, and had departed LGA about 2 minutes before the in-flight event occurred. The 150 passengers and 5 crewmembers evacuated the airplane via the forward and overwing exits.

AIR CRASH INVESTIGATIONS

GHOSTS?

The Crash of Eastern Air Lines Flight 401

On December 29, 1972, an Eastern Air Lines' Lockheed L-1011, as Flight 401 on its way from John F. Kennedy International Airport, New York, to Miami International Airport, Miami, Florida, crashed at 2342 EST in the Everglades, just westnorthwest of Miami International Airport. The aircraft was destroyed. From the 176 people on board 101 people died in the crash.

Pete Collins, Editor

On December 29, 1972 an Eastern Air Lines' Lockheed L-1011, as Flight 401 on its way from John F. Kennedy International Airport, New York, to Miami International Airport, Miami, Florida, crashed at 2342 EST in the Everglades, just westnorthwest of Miami International Airport. The aircraft was destroyed, 99 people 99 died in the crash. The flight had problems with the nose landing gear. The National Transportation Safety Board determines that the probable cause of this accident, was that preoccupation with a malfunction distracted the crew and allowed the descent to go unnoticed.

Printed in Great Britain
by Amazon

53019347R00056